Praise for The Path To Freedom

"It's a grim reality for so many entrepreneurs - the business they built to give them freedom becomes the shackles that prevent them from achieving the very freedom they covet. Barry's book cuts through all the business 'how-to' noise as he skillfully weaves the deeper truths of our humanness into a practical guide that any entrepreneur can use to build a business that truly runs without them. Read this book, apply the lessons and achieve what most entrepreneurs never will!"

-- Miranda Hill

THE PATH TO FREEDOM

THE PATH
TO FREEDOM

**The 9 Steps to Create a Highly
Profitable Business That Runs
Without You**

Barry Williame Magliarditi

Founder and CEO, The Game Changers

THE PATH TO FREEDOM

This book is dedicated to the entrepreneurs and business owners whom I have been called to serve: my "Game Changers." You inspire me each and every day and have made it possible for me to do this fulfilling work that I love. This book is a culmination of the last 18 years of my life in business, and the result of many failures and learning things the hard way. This book also stands as proof that regardless of your background, upbringing, race or religion, you to have within you the ability to build your own Path To Freedom. If this book helps you overcome even one of the many challenges we face in business every day and enables you to enjoy the process more, then this will have been a success. I see you and your greatness, let this book be the key that unlocks that.

CONTENTS

Why is mindset so important?

Where do beliefs come from?

How to resolve limiting beliefs

Understanding self-sabotage

Reptilian brain neurology

Building your intuition

Changing your mindset

Developing your personal power

Your responsibility as an entrepreneur

Stepping up and leaning in

Where to from here?

Foreword

As I sit here drinking my cacao writing this, I'm snuggled up at home where my wife just gave birth to our second child. A beautiful girl, Ayva who just turned five weeks.

I share this because we were able to take a couple of months off from business activities and enjoy the baby bubble knowing our multi-million dollar enterprise is humming away, making sales, supporting our staff, and supporting our life.

However, this wasn't always the case. Just two and a half years earlier we had our first son. My wife Kristie and I literally worked right up until she was in labor, and we were back in the trenches doing back-to-back sales calls, team meetings, and other trainings within two days after he was born.

It was hectic. We were overwhelmed by the business which felt like it was out of control. We were making more money than we had ever imagined (our core business is actually helping people to create more money, freedom, and impact online)... but everything depended on us.

Barely any systems, no clear direction... everything relied on our decisions. This equalled zero freedom. But freedom is why we get into business in the first place, right?

I'm honored to write the forward for this book for my friend Barry, because he's been a huge catalyst for me in my business journey. I remember when I first met him, I was dating a girl and he was dating her best friend, so we ended up spending a weekend together on the northern beaches of Sydney.

It was early in my entrepreneurial journey. I was struggling to get traction and hit the income goals I dreamed of. During a board game called The Wish, Barry with his NLP coaching expertise helped activate something within me. Within weeks I had quadrupled my sales volume and started really accelerating things in my ability to create results in business.

We lived on opposite sides of Australia, but we stayed in touch. And every time we talked, Barry would inspire me to go to the next level of what I was capable of and create a business that reflected that. During the last year, working with him and his team has helped my wife and me to see that we didn't have solid foundations in place for our business. This meant we were capped in terms of time, money, and most importantly, freedom.

The bottom line was, although we had a successful and profitable business we really didn't have the freedom to really enjoy it. Without laying the right foundations, getting the right team, and putting the right systems in place... we'd be forever stuck on the entrepreneurial hamster wheel.

Now, I'm a visionary. I had so many ideas and projects to implement, but I just didn't have the capacity nor the bandwidth to start or create anything new. We were lacking a supportive team and the structure required to implement and execute these ideas, which became super frustrating.

I knew we were leaving so much opportunity and money on the table. I knew I needed systems but I just didn't know what to do.

Fortunately I knew Barry!

What you'll find here in this book is a roadmap to a business and mission that can run with or without you.

Now if you're anything like me, you don't want to just create a business so you don't have to work in it, or just sit on a beach drinking Pina Coladas. You want to make a difference. You want to leave a legacy. You want to create something meaningful and make a positive impact to the planet and the people living on it...

And you love what you do. Yet, you don't want to be a slave to it. You want to run it, not for it to run you. You want to be inspired by it, not ruled by it.

In my opinion, the ultimate goal is having a business that runs profitably with or without you, which then gives you the choice to do what inspires you the most within that business. It could be leading up marketing ideas, doing sales calls, writing content, training a team, creating video content, or just coming up with innovative ideas.

Whatever your passion and inspiration are, it's possible for you to have a business that gives you the freedom, the time, and space to work within it how you see fit. A business that aligns with your values and gives you the time and space to be in or away from it if you wish. That's freedom, and that's possible for you.

That's what Barry has so elegantly laid out in this book.

Now it's not a quick fix, and it's not easy... but you didn't become an entrepreneur because it's easy! If you're willing to do the groundwork, and really apply yourself, follow the steps in the book you'll be well on your way of creating a business that is fulfilling for you, your staff, and your family on all levels.

We're at a crucial turning point here on the planet. There is a serious restructure that is happening, and it's you, the entrepreneurs, that will create the businesses, and in turn the ways of transacting, trading, selling, and inspiring that will lead this planet into the new economy and the new way of being - in fairness, equality, prosperity, abundance, and love.

There's never been a more important time for us to step up into our full potential, and to lead and create what is in our heart and soul.

Don't let this book be another book that just sits on the shelf, or that you read but don't implement. There is literally tens of thousands of dollars worth of information in here and years of trial and error... but it's worthless if you don't apply it.

Barry, you're a legend brother. I'm truly grateful to call you a friend. Thank you for who you are, for impacting mine and Kristie's life, and for going first, for always seeing the best in people, and for impacting thousands - and the ripple of millions - with your presence and the message right here in the words of this book.

With Love,

Clint X Morgan.

Preface

Freedom. I didn't fully get the concept until 24 hours ago when I was released from my detainment cell.

I'm writing this having just returned to Australia from Bali international airport immigration where I've been held for days without food, water, or basic necessities.

How did I end up in this hellish situation? I was in the middle of writing a book about freedom. How had I suddenly had my own freedom stripped away from me so suddenly?

On 14th of May 2020 in the midst of COVID-19 I was on a flight back to Bali, the place I've called home for the last few months. I was flying back after returning to Australia to spend school holidays with my two boys, Leo and Zave.

I felt lucky to be on this flight. While I was in Australia holidaying with my boys, I knew there was a strong possibility I'd be stuck in Australia for much longer than the 3 week trip I'd planned. There were no flights to Bali during the extreme border restrictions and overall pandemic chaos that was happening around the world.

While planning my return to Bali, I approached a visa company that had been recommended by a friend. The company promised they could get me a KITAS (long stay visa) which would allow me easier and longer-term access to Indonesia without the required 'visa run' flights every 30-60 days.

Grateful to have found this company, I paid them and received my KITAS. School holidays concluded, my boys went back to school and I patiently awaited a flight back to my newly adopted home in Indonesia.

I ensured I had all the appropriate documentation for a smooth transit including a COVID-19 test result and doctor's certification I was coronavirus-free.

Leaving Australia and getting through border control presented some challenges. But they were nothing compared to landing in Denpasar the evening of the 14th of May, proceeding through immigration, and being stopped for not having the appropriate stamp in my passport.

I was swiftly escorted to a small room inside the immigration facility and told to wait.

Hours passed. What was going on?

Eventually I was told that my KITAS wasn't registered. I found myself being ushered by three men late at night into a small hallway in the departures area. That was where I would spend my first sleepless, anxious night.

I had no food, no water, and no idea what was going on. All I knew was that I wasn't even allowed to go to the bathroom without an escort.

The second day proved no better. I was put into a small room with no furniture, no food, and no water. Nobody would give me any information. So again I waited.

Twenty-four hours later, I received my first meal along with the news that I was to be deported back to Australia on the next available flight. The next available flight was 14 days later… so I was to stay in my cell until then.

Facing 14 days in a cell without basic necessities… It was a lot to process.

I tried to come to terms with my situation. I was in a cell in another country, with no bed, no food or water, and no clue as to what had gone so horribly wrong in what was to be my return to my new home in paradise.

The air conditioner blasted cold air into my cell day and night. I spent my time thinking, meditating, and trying to sleep while shivering on the icy-cold concrete floor.

Fortunately, I was allowed to use my mobile phone. I called my visa company. They told me there had been a mistake and I would be let out that day.

But when the promised release time came and went, I started to realize I needed to take things into my own hands.

I reached out to everyone in my network who might be able to find out what was going on and help me get the hell out of that cell.

News came back that I could pay 35 million rupiahs (about $3,500 Australian dollars) to buy my way out. I proceeded with that option, only to receive further promises and delays. I was stuck.

On day three I discovered my landlord in Bali used to run a large immigration company and was very well connected. I got into contact with him, and he promised he'd find out what he could.

Shit was about to get real...

I found out that I'd been sold a fraudulent KITAS with the code of a recently deceased Chinese woman.

A simple visa mix-up had turned into full-scale fraud.

I was in big, big trouble.

Throughout the entire experience, it had felt so surreal and disconnected from the incredible life I'd been living earlier. It was hard to believe that only a few days ago, I'd been so excited to return home to Bali and see my friends and loved ones again.

Now I was facing long-term imprisonment in a foreign country.

But while this situation was playing out, something incredible happened.

I felt that things were going to be ok. Or rather, I chose to feel this way. I meditated. I did yoga. I sat in gratitude for the life I had lived, knowing that whatever came next would be a part of my journey... but it wouldn't be my whole journey.

Because no single one moment defines who we are. In every situation, we can choose how we respond. We can choose our path.

Also another experience happened that was so unique and beautiful I'm now doubting whether it was meant to happen in any other way…

I had been building a friendship with a girl I'd never met in person. Through Zoom dates and long phone calls, we'd been building a beautiful connection in a way I had never experienced before. We'd been sharing our vulnerabilities, hopes and dreams, forging a divine connection without ever touching or having met face to face.

Part of why I had been so excited to return to Bali was so I could meet her in person for the first time. We had arranged our first meeting for the day after I got back.

Despite not wanting her to worry about me, we had committed to 100% open communication, so I knew I had to tell her what had happened to me. So I texted her from my detention cell to let her know why I couldn't make it.

With approval from my guards, she arranged to bring food over - a smorgasbord of my favourite dishes - and rushed to see me. This certainly wasn't the meeting either of us had planned, but sometimes the universe has other experiences planned for us.

As fate would have it, we spent our first (and only) 10 minutes of face-to-face time in a detention cell in Bali airport.

Life's most beautiful moments can happen in the strangest of places.

I'll tell you the outcome of my immigration scare in a minute…

But first it's time to address something really important.

Something has led you to purchase this book.

Maybe it's the promise of making more money.

Maybe it's the promise of having more time.

Maybe it's the promise of truly living a life of freedom.

Or maybe it's some form of inner guidance that has led you to these pages.

Regardless of what led you here, you're about to embark on a journey that will change your life forever.

This book contains not only the defined steps to build a business that can work without you, make you more money, and provide you the freedom you seek… this book will also give you the inner guidance to change your life.

I believe business is a personal and spiritual journey back to one's true self. Being in business will bring up everything that's blocking you from living an extraordinary life.

Don't be surprised if, as you read and implement what's shared here, that you start to see significant changes not only in your business, but within yourself.

Our clients always report that 'we've made more money, and have more time, but one thing we never expected is that every area of our life has improved in ways we never thought possible.'

This is not a book to simply set up systems within your business. It's a book to break you free from the old paradigm of the systems you've unknowingly abided by for so long - the systems that have been stopping you from having it all. From being all of who you are.

If this is sounding a little woo-woo… maybe so, but that doesn't mean it's not true. But I'll leave that for you to decide for yourself after you've read the book and implemented what I've shared in these pages.

Getting back to my near-miss with Indonesian immigration…

Through deep trust in my heart, and following my inner guidance, I found a lawyer who successfully negotiated my release with zero marks on my immigration file (at a hefty price tag I might add). I received a ticket back to Australia where I could apply once more to return, this time under a legitimate KITAS.

Today, thinking about this lesson in liberty, I am grateful for the experience.

Because it confirmed to me exactly what I have been writing about in this book.

Thanks to where I am in my business, I had the cash available to pay nearly $20k in fines to various levels of Indonesian immigration. I have a network of people who can help me solve different types of problems. And I was able to disappear for a few days and know that everything was running smoothly without me.

If I hadn't followed the steps within this book to get where I am now in my business journey, I might still be stuck in that cell. Or I would be stuck in another prison of my own making... a business that demanded everything of me.

I think that COVID-19 has shown all of us that we don't actually have much control over what happens to us in the bigger sense. One minute we can be riding high and the next the rug can be pulled out from under us.

The external world is chaotic. But that doesn't mean we cannot learn to ride the waves and live how we choose.

Freedom exists within ourselves.

I feel that the path to freedom is knowing who you really are, expressing that authentically, being connected to your heart, and being able to clearly listen to and follow that guidance.

That is the purpose of life, and everything else is a bonus.

You can create whatever you want in this world. You can have your cake and eat it too.

You won't always get what you want, and it won't always be easy. But you will absolutely get the experience you need for your growth. And that goes far beyond money and time... but by applying the principles you'll learn in this book, you'll get those too.

Here's to changing your game and following your path to true freedom.

Barry 'true freedom' Magliarditi

Acknowledgements

I want to start by acknowledging and thanking all the kids who picked on me in school. The ones who beat me up. The ones who beat me down. The ones who called me names. And the ones who said I'd never amount to anything.

You didn't know it then, and it probably wasn't your intention, but you gave me an incredible gift. You taught me resilience and toughened me up at a very young age. You prepared me for the knocks, disappointments, and hardships of life in business. So when challenges inevitably came along, I was already conditioned to push through and keep fighting. Thank you.

Thank you to all the teachers I had throughout the years who told me I'd go nowhere in life, who told me I couldn't read or write properly, and that so many of my skills were below standard when I was a kid. You gave me the encouragement to prove you wrong and be all of who I was meant to be.

To my past girlfriends and partners in intimate relationships I've had, thank you for helping me finally realize that love isn't something that is outside of me... it's something that is already inside of me. All of our breakups, however painful, took me on another step in my own journey to giving and receiving love as fully as I can.

To Trinity, the mother of our two amazing boys Leo and Zave, thank you for always being a fantastic mother to them. Although things didn't work out with us the way we'd once intended, I appreciate and respect the fact that you've seen my dream and my vision, and have done your best to support me to achieve it.

And thank you for stepping up to be our boys' caregiver at times when I haven't been physically around to help you and give you the support you needed. Our kids inspire me to achieve bigger and bigger dreams. They show me that anything is possible, and I trust I've given them the same gift.

I want to thank my two sons, Leo and Zave for being an inspiration. You're a direct reflection of my own inner child, highlighting areas where I needed to love myself and heal myself. Knowing you both, and watching you grow into incredible young men, gives me the strength and the spark to be the best I can be, and help as many people as I can.

To my past partner Jess, you played such a pivotal role in my development within myself. You showed me compassion and love, and through that experience, you taught me who I really was. You taught me the importance of self-esteem and self-confidence, of having (and giving) love and support, and of what's possible in unity. I'm forever grateful for the impact that you've had within my life and within The Game Changers business and its clients.

Thank you to my mum and dad for always providing the best they possibly could over the years. And thank you mum and dad for believing in me. It hasn't always been a smooth road, but I'm grateful for the challenges and support I received, even when you didn't necessarily understand what I was doing!

Thank you mum for showing me compassion and love, and for showing me sacrifice in what you did to bring up my three brothers and me. Thank you dad for teaching me leadership. Thank you for showing me how to be hard and kind at the same time. I'll be forever grateful for the lessons you've taught me.

To my grandfather, thank you for teaching me that family is important, and so is hard work. Your teachings, words and wisdom still ripple through me.

Uncle Chris, thank you for always being there, and making yourself available to give me your time and your love. By helping me to work on my many projects at the farm, you helped allow me to flourish creatively and think differently - something that has been incredibly important in my entrepreneurial journey.

To my brothers Thomas, James, and Nick I appreciate the journey we share together and the stories and memories we've created that still bring a laugh during family gatherings - and also reflections and disbelief on making it this far!

It wouldn't be an acknowledgement without giving tribute to my first coach and dear friend, Mihir Thaker. We connected shortly after my bankruptcy when a passion was awoken in me and I was feeling called to serve humanity. You were the one person that was always able to hold a bigger frame and vision for me than I ever was able to see for myself. As our friendship grew, you also created a space for me to finally experience deep friendship and trust. You created an opening that allowed me to start accessing my vulnerability. I will always cherish the time and journey we shared, which was deep and profound to say the least. It was much shorter than myself and many others who knew you would have prayed for. I know and trust that wherever your spirit is, it had a greater purpose to fulfill than here on Earth. RIP brother.

Thank you to Kori for giving me the gift of feeling seen, of being heard, and giving me the freedom and safety to explore who I am in our friendship. Thank you for allowing me to share my vulnerability in a space where I am not judged or needing to be fixed, but just to be me. Thank you for accepting all of who I am, and for providing me with the space to see all of you, too.

To my entire team at The Game Changers, each and every one of you inspire me every day. I'm so grateful that we get the opportunity to travel through life together, and create the impact that we are having on so many clients across the world - to help them have more money, more time, and connect with themselves in a deeper and more fulfilling way. I love, appreciate and respect every one of you and without you this wouldn't be possible or carry the same meaning.

Thank you team also for helping me decide on a title, book cover, and other aspects of this project.

To the many clients I've worked with throughout the years, I am so grateful for the opportunities I've had to work with you and gain feedback through your businesses that helps me assist other businesses to grow. Without you I wouldn't be anywhere near the blessed position I find myself in here in 2020. The impact I've been able to create has been because of your trust in me, your support of me, and your love of the vision of The Game Changers. I'm forever grateful for you, your staff, and your families - you're all part of my family now too.

A huge thank you to Sam Wallis who's been by my side for years, helping share my message and our teaching to the world through your incredible copywriting skills. Without you and your dedication to me and this work, this book would still be years of knowledge stuck in my head. The process of extracting this information from my head and heart and compiling it into this book is masterful and I'll be forever grateful for your patience, persistence, passion, and belief in me. Thank you.

I also want to thank ME for never giving up. For getting up every time I got knocked down. For the perseverance, determination, and willingness to face the challenges and hard times with humility, pride, love, and trust that I would get through it. And not just get through it, but get through it for the better and use my experiences to serve others so they don't have to go through the hard experiences I have in their own businesses.

And of course, I want to thank my many mentors that have had a huge impact on my life.

Irmansyah Effendi, we met again at the perfect time on my spiritual journey when I was ready to remember who I am and what I'm here to do. Your teachings around the heart have impacted my life and others who I, in turn, impact with your teachings.

To my previous NLP teachers - Sharon Pearson, Joe Pane, Carl Buchheit, and Michelle Masters, you taught me so much around psychology, and helped me understand that my beliefs and how I am wired is an important part of my being, and that my thoughts and language create my reality.

To the various business mentors who have influenced me along the way after reading your books, listening to your podcasts, or attending your seminars… you've all contributed to my experience of entrepreneurialism and helped me get where I am today. You've helped me to share all I have to share with my clients to help them grow as well. I've learned something from all of your combined wisdom and experience, much of which is reflected in this book.

And to my ex-boss Philip who rang to abuse me and tell me I was hopeless and should 'just quit life now'… I'd like to say a big Thank you. Without that experience I may have never felt the call to start my own business and be where I'm at now.

Lastly, to all past, present and future lessons, leaders, and lovers, thank you.

I honor you. I appreciate you. I see you.

INTRODUCTION

INTRODUCTION

"Between stimulus and response, there is a space. In that space is our power to choose our response. In our response lies our growth and our freedom."

- Vicktor Emil Frankl

These days, more people are running their own businesses than ever before.

All over the world, entrepreneurs are paving their own way professionally, aiming to become self-sufficient enough to live their dream lifestyle, with the freedom to do what they've always wanted.

Yet somehow only a fraction of businesses make it past 5 years. Even less actually end up giving the business owner the lifestyle they initially set out to achieve.

Why is this so?

The answer is surprisingly simple… and yet we make it complex.

Until we systemize our business so it can run without us, we'll always be our own employee. Oftentimes, that means being paid the least and working the most hours - despite the flashy title of CEO!

What's worse, a business that cannot run without you is a high-risk game to play. If you spend your days fixing emergencies, answering questions, and guiding staff… your business has a single point of failure: You.

That means you're risking your income, your family's income, and your employees' income too. If you cannot work for a period of time, people lose their livelihoods. That's not fair on anyone, and it's no way to live either.

Because you've picked up this book, I can tell you want to unchain yourself from your business and gain the freedom to live your dream lifestyle. At the very least, you're curious about a better way to run things. So you can earn more, work less, and actually enjoy being in business again.

Either way, congratulations on taking the first step towards systemizing your business so that it runs - and grows - whether you're around or not.

This is the beginning of your journey on the Path to Freedom.

By the end of this book, you'll understand the exact steps required for building a business that works without you. You can realistically implement all 9 steps and start seeing rapid growth and profit while working 1-2 days less in your business… all within the next 6-12 months.

Let me make one thing clear - just because you *can* step out of your business doesn't mean you *have* to.

You probably love what you do. You don't want to do anything else. I'm not saying you should run away and abandon all responsibility - far from it. Besides, let's be honest, sitting on a beach sipping Margaritas sounds nice for a few days… but after a week you'd be going crazy with boredom.

Because you're an entrepreneur. You love the challenges and triumphs of running your own business. I get it - because I feel the same way.

Just because I have largely removed myself from the operations of my business doesn't mean that I'm sitting around doing nothing. Far from it. In fact, I'm more productive now than ever. I just focus on different things than back when my life was all about the hustle and grind.

My point is this: A business that runs without you gives you *the freedom of choice.* You can choose to work in it, on it, or on another project you're passionate about. But *you have the power to choose.*

To me, that is freedom.

In this book, you'll find both insight and action. You'll learn things you might not have known before. You'll be challenged to think about things in a different way. Most of all, you'll be prompted to take action on what you've learned.

Because information means nothing unless you do something about it.

I want this book to be your personal Path to Freedom. I designed it to be a practical guide for getting your business self-sufficient at a much faster pace than trying to figure things out on your own. Inside you'll find the knowledge and tools to realize your dream lifestyle much sooner than you think is possible.

Once you achieve autonomy within your business, you can then take your skillset into any venture, any business … and do it in half the time again.

Success leaves a path that's more easily followed the second, third, and fourth times.

Right now, it might be a stretch for you to imagine a future where you don't actually have to 'work'. Let me tell you, now that you're reading this book, that future isn't as unachievable - or far away - as you may think.

As I'm writing down these notes right now, I'm sitting in an airport lounge about to begin a 6-month trip through Asia, feeling calm and secure in the knowledge that my business is totally taken care of.

It will keep running without me. Leads will keep coming in, and the right ones will be converted into clients. Members of my business growth program The Opulence System™ will continue to get all the coaching and support they need to achieve rapid, scalable growth.

I can relax knowing that my team at The Game Changers are fully capable and empowered to handle any hiccups along the way - they don't need to run to me for answers. Even more than that, they are driven to ensure that my business actually grows and improves while I'm away.

I want this level of freedom for you.

It took me 5 years to go from coaching 1:1 clients in rented offices to where I am now, at the helm of a multimillion-dollar organization that's changing lives. I did it the hard way, figuring everything out largely on my own. I have also had the guidance of some brilliant mentors. Their wisdom will echo through the pages you're about to read.

Using the steps to freedom outlined in this book, you can transform your business in less than 12 months. It doesn't matter what industry you're in. At The Game Changers, our coaching clients come from all walks of life. Bookkeeping. Concreting. Graphic design. Life coaching. Plumbing. Martial Arts training. Real estate.

In all these industries, members still typically achieve 3-6x times growth, free up 10+ hours a week and take their first big holiday in years, all within their first 6-12 months with us.

So read this book, and commit to implementing what you learn straight away for rapid, scalable, and sustainable growth.

I know you're keen to get started. But before we begin, we must first look at the most important factor in making it all work.

The missing piece of the puzzle

There's no other time in history where we have had so much access to information. You can pick up your smartphone and Google how to do literally anything in seconds.

So why then do 3 out of 4 businesses still fail?

It's because information is only one side of the equation. Without recalibrating our mindset with the right settings to actually take action on what we learn (and to stay consistent in those actions)... *nothing changes.*

Think about it. Each year, millions of people make New Years' resolutions, but they typically last just 3 weeks before we fall into the same behavior patterns as before. We know smoking causes cancer. But one billion people worldwide still smoke. We know that eating healthy food and exercising regularly is the key to maintaining a healthy weight. Yet obesity is still a global health crisis.

Without getting into a deeper discussion about the nature of addiction, let's just agree that motivating ourselves to act is the hardest part of creating lasting change.

In short: Knowing doesn't equal doing.

That's why this book will also focus on helping you develop the mindset you'll need to implement the behaviors that will help you reach your goals.

The Opulence System™ members get regular 1:1 and group coaching sessions. Obviously, I can't give you that through a book. But what I can do is introduce you to some new concepts, and ask some different questions that are designed to get you thinking about your own behaviors and the triggers behind them.

With that in mind, let me introduce you to the first mindset shift you need to make.

The #1 reason most businesses fail

The reality is you need very little to succeed.

The fundamentals of business and marketing haven't changed in 100 years. There's just more noise around to confuse and distract you.

Applying these fundamentals is not difficult. Is it hard work? In the beginning, yes. But it's not rocket science.

The most important factor in any business' success isn't strategy or tactics. Sure, they are both important. But the single thing that will determine your success or failure is your mindset.

To succeed in business, you need to be constantly upgrading your mindset to play at higher levels of the game.

Because your business will never outgrow you. It will never expand beyond your capability as a business owner.

Let me explain.

My firm belief is that we never have business problems. We have personal problems that get expressed through our business.

Clients walking over you? It's likely that you don't value yourself enough to set healthy boundaries.

Failing to attract good staff? It's likely that you are playing out unhelpful relationship dynamics instead of being the leader they need.

Unable to break through your current glass ceiling of revenue? It's likely that you are subconsciously uncomfortable with earning more than your parents or peers.

Working ridiculous hours a week? It's likely that deep down you are trying to prove yourself worthy of success.

Our underlying mindset and belief system *always* create our experience of life. On an unconscious level, we get what we ask for.

Now, if you're in a crappy position right now, I'm not saying that you are happy to be there.

Because you're reading this book, I can already tell you're driven, ambitious, and probably pretty frustrated that your business isn't what you want it to be.

But on some level, you are comfortable with whatever level you're playing at. Because you are familiar with it. There are no surprises. Nothing you cannot cope with (at least for now). No chance of being 'found out' (we'll talk more about impostor syndrome later). In a counter-productive kind of way... you feel safe.

Here's why.

Transformational NLP (Neuro-Linguistic Programming) expert Carl Buchheit Ph.D. once said that *the experiences we learn to survive become the experiences our ongoing survival depends upon.*

If we've survived experiences of poverty, of poor relationships, of poor health, and so on... it's easier for us to endure those things because they've been self-programmed as 'survivable' and therefore 'safe' experiences.

Even though we know logically that having more money, being single, or making healthier lifestyle choices are not unsafe experiences... the little primal critter holds us back from stepping into the unknown. Which stops us from growing into the person we need to be to get the things we really want.

You might think this little critter is annoying and should be squashed. Don't be too hard on it. It's trying to look out for you. It's obsessed with a singular goal: your survival.

To ensure our survival, our primal critter brain has two main functions:

1. Keeping us safe from danger (real or perceived)

It's been a long time since we had to protect ourselves from the saber-tooth tiger. Yet our critter brain is still hell-bent on saving us from risk. It does everything it can to maintain the status quo. Even if the status quo is limiting our growth.

Want to explore what's on the other side of that hill? Woah there, kiddo... we don't know what's over there. It could be dangerous. Best to not venture far from your cave.

Nowadays this scenario looks more like -

Want to land that next-level big client? That's a whole lot more responsibility and risk that you're used to, pal. You might fail to deliver on your promises. Your business could collapse. Your wife will leave you and your children will laugh at you. Better sabotage that meeting and stay in your lane. Phew, that was a close one buddy. Good thing I'm here to keep you safe.

Making sure we keep belonging to our tribe

2. Most animals survive by banding together in social groups to share food, shelter, and protection. We humans are no different. Our family dynamics, experiences in school, socioeconomic environment, and a multitude of other factors all contribute to the social identity we develop to cement our place in the 'tribe' as we grow up.

   As adults, we fight to remain consistent with that identity. The 'battler'. The 'underdog'. The 'chubby one'. The 'class clown'.

   At some point in our childhood or young adulthood, these identities helped us survive. But although these identities aren't serving us any more... deep down we unconsciously still hold onto them. That is until we start to question them and replace our old limiting beliefs with better ones.

Basically, many business owners experience constant internal friction between their ambition and their desire for safety and belonging. Until you upgrade our social identity and belief systems to embrace growth and change, you'll keep sabotaging your success to keep yourself tucked up in your 'safe' place.

Call it fear of failure. Call it fear of success. Call it just plain pig-headedness… whatever. It's time to set yourself free from it.

Your first steps forward

You may be wondering what all this has to do with running a business.

"I picked up this book to learn secret ninja hacks and supercharge my business, Barry. What the hell?"

We'll get to the meaty action later. But make no mistake - you cannot ignore this 'mindset stuff' and still expect the results you want.

It's real. It's the reason you've read The E-Myth, attended workshops, listened to podcasts, took a marketing course, and whatever else, yet you still find yourself doing the same things… and getting the same results.

I get that you're frustrated. That you probably feel like you should be further along in business than you are now. Maybe you're even wondering if it's all even worth it. Because you're paying a huge price. You're not getting the time you want for your family, your friends or for your own self-care.

You're stuck in your business… and it doesn't want to let you go.

If this is all starting to sound a bit heavy - don't panic.

This book is organized so that you'll take the right steps in the right order to start building a stronger and more independent framework for your business.

Systems and processes, KPIs and goals, hiring and retaining an A-player team... it's all not as hard as you may think it is. Not when you know the frameworks and specifics around setting the right processes up.

I'll show you how. And I'll also give you resources to help you on your way.

One last thing…

If you're like 99% of the entrepreneurs I meet, you've got a lot of emotion tied up in your business. It's like your baby. But right now it's kind of like a bawling toddler. It constantly wants your attention. Every time it falls down you have to pick it up. If you don't feed it, it suffers.

As nice as it is to feel needed… it's time to let go and help your baby thrive. It's time to grow up.

By the end of this book, you'll know how to raise your business from a bawling toddler through teenage-hood (with minimal tantrums and sullen silences), and give it the foundations it needs to become a self-sufficient and productive adult.

Before we get started, I want you to agree to have an open mind about what you're about to read. At times, you will feel resistance. Your primal brain critter will tell you things like:

'That won't work for my business.'

'I can't do that because…'

'Yeah, but my business is different because…'

When you hear those negative thoughts, just remember it's your little brain critter trying to keep you 'safe' in the same situation you're in right now. So thank it for its advice, but tell it you're here to learn a new way forward.

A quick trip through time: from then to now

I went into business with one clear goal: I didn't want to create the experience I had growing up.

My father worked hard to earn enough to take care of us. Despite his good intentions, what this translated as for myself and my siblings, was a largely absent father.

So I grew up following the same path - with the same beliefs - that I had learned growing up:

Work hard, earn money, and one day maybe you can retire. Then you can start really living… but only if you've managed to save enough money by then.

So I started my working life, as most people do, as an employee.

My boss back then was a jerk who thrived on belittling those around him. And one day in my mid-20s, I had had enough.

I decided I'd build my own business. Figuring that if I worked my butt off for a few years, it would eventually give me the time and money to do whatever I wanted. So I could be there for my kids like my father wasn't there for me and my siblings.

Plus, I loved the idea of being in control of my own enterprise. When I was the boss, I could call the shots. I would be at nobody's beck and call. It sounded good. Because like every other entrepreneur, I had a rebellious streak inside me that hated being told what to do.

My own business would equal freedom and wealth. All it would take is a few years of hard work, then I'd be set up for a great life. What could go wrong?

Three weeks later I put an ad in the paper:

Handyman services. No job too big or small.
Soon enough, the phone started ringing. Long story short, that was the beginning of my first company - a kitchen and bathroom installation business.

Five years later, I was working in my own factory with 15 staff and a multi-million dollar turnover.

I'd made it, right?

Wrong.

Ironically, I had created the exact same experience for my kids that I had growing up. I was totally absent. I worked 80+ hours a week and got home too late to even put them to bed.

What's worse… I had created even MORE of the very situation I was trying to avoid.

I was working more hours that my dad did. I was not present when I was home. I was tired and stressed all the time. And I didn't have any money, because every cent was invested in growing this business that was already way out of hand.

As a result, my relationships suffered not just with my kids, but with my partner too.

I know now that because I grew up in that environment, I was programmed to seek that familiar experience. But I didn't know that then. So I thought the answer was 'just work harder'. More hours. More staff. More clients.

But all that did was add volume to the same problems I already had.

So eventually it all collapsed, and I went bankrupt to the tune of $1.2 million dollars. Around that same time, my partner left me and took the kids. I lost everything.

Looking back now, I consider this an enormous gift. (Although it was gut-wrenchingly painful at the time).

Because after everything fell apart, I had to stop and think 'how did I stuff things up so badly?'.

Losing everything gave me a reason to find a better way to live, both professionally and personally. I was determined to pick myself up and start again. But next time I was going to do things differently.

So I looked for answers everywhere I possibly could. I read books on business, economics, marketing, leadership, personal development. I sought advice from mentors who had successfully created the results I wanted. I immersed myself in seminars, courses and masterminds.

Sometime later, I started coaching.

At first, it was a side hustle. I never imagined I would end up as a business coach. I coached all sorts of people on their phobias, fears, depression and other issues that people seek guidance from life coaches for.

Six months later, I realized that I was mostly attracting business owners as clients... and they were all starting to report amazing business growth since working with me.

I wondered… how could my clients be creating these incredible new results in their business, when all we were doing was working on themselves?

This helped me make the connection between what's going on INSIDE (your mindset and beliefs) and how it affects EVERY other part of your life, including how you run your business, and the consequential results you get.

I got curious about how what I was doing with them from a mindset perspective was affecting their business growth. As they made changes in their mindset and beliefs, things would shift and unblock not just personally but professionally.

This was my first Game Changer moment.

It's when I realized that we never have business problems, we have personal problems that show up in our business.

After a couple of years of getting results for my clients, I pivoted into business coaching and started The Game Changers. Now that I had repeated proof that I could affect real positive change in business, I knew it was time to bring it to a wider audience.

Fast forward to now and The Game Changers is a multimillion-dollar organization that helps business owners gain back control, triple their profits and double their time off in 12 months or less. Visit this page to see some of our amazing client feedback: https://www.thegamechangers.com.au/game-changers/

Thanks to the steps I've put in place, and my incredible A-team who drive the business for me, my business works without me being there to run it. I'm free to spend quality time with my kids, explore new countries, dedicate time to charity organizations, and basically do what I please.

I'm about to show you how to do the same.

I'm going to teach you the nine steps to systemize your business. You can realistically implement them all into your business over the next 90 days and start seeing incredible results fast.

Yes, they take work. But they're not rocket science. They're based on the practical experience and knowledge from the best business minds over the last 50 years.

The only thing that will stop you from implementing is what's between your ears.

I don't mean your intelligence - you don't need to be a genius to follow the simple steps I will outline to you. What I mean is the behavioral changes with your mindset and decision making.

You need to create a growth mindset. To be open to new ideas (even if they sound a bit woo-woo at first). Be comfortable with being uncomfortable. Trust in what you cannot see yet. And ask for help along the way.

I promise you all will be revealed at the right time. No bongo-drum circle or henna tattoos required. (But feel free to bring them along, if that's your thing.)

THE PATH TO FREEDOM

YOUR VISION

YOUR VISION

"Defining my vision has allowed me to do things I've been talking about for 10 years. Because now I can align people behind me who want to help me achieve it."

Haami Williams
WireCon Concreting Services

"If I was still working like I was 18 months ago, I'd be in an institution."

My eyes widened. I knew Haami was serious. Sitting in his office in Geelong, surrounded by lists and papers and other office paraphernalia, for a minute I saw the guy who had been drowning in his business when I first met him. Then he cracked his massive, generous smile.

Haami is a big guy with a big personality.

An ex-AFL player (that's Australian Rules football to my non-Aussie friends), Haami has a strong presence. He's a natural leader who radiates warmth with a no-nonsense vibe.

Haami built his concreting business through sheer hard work. He is fuelled by the same spark I see in most entrepreneurs - a willingness to work 80+ hour weeks and always be ready for more.

In the fourth year in business, Haami hit $4 million in turnover. That number looks pretty good in print... but he was running a team of 25 guys, as well as working on jobs himself too.

Haami's workday started at 3.30 am with a pre-dawn drive to a worksite. In the afternoon he'd drive back to the office to organize jobs, people, and paperwork. At midnight, he'd sneak back through his front door, too late to see his kids or kiss his wife goodnight.

"Things were literally out of control, Barry. They were really tough times."

Now, Haami is a guy who's always been physically active. He's always been involved with sport and enjoys challenging himself. He's even done the Kokoda trail - twice! "I can still run rings around the young blokes in my company."

But the grind was wearing him down.

Haami didn't have any vision that informed his direction in his business. He simply worked his guts out. No matter which direction he was pointing in, Haami would give 150% to moving forward in that direction.

"Before I had a vision to work towards, I was just focused on making money for its own sake. If we made more than we spent, that was a good month. Eventually, I realized that by going into business, I'd just bought myself a job."

This highlights a particular nasty pitfall of working without a vision. Without having a clear idea of where you're going, you never get anywhere in particular. You work, you earn, you spend. Rinse and repeat.

What are you doing it all for?

Most business owners avoid creating a compelling vision for their business.

Why?

Because it has no immediate ROI. It doesn't directly bring in any money. And especially in the startup phase (making less than $1.2 million per year in revenue), cashflow drivers such as marketing or sales seem much more important endeavors.

Creating a vision? Pfft! I don't have time for that stuff. I've got a business to run!

What if I told you this was a flawed assumption? A problem that could cost you millions?

The critical mindset shift that could save your business

Most people start their working life as an employee. We go to work for someone else, they tell us what to do, and we collect money for our labor.

The shadow of this 'work equals reward' mindset often remains entrenched in our subconscious belief system. For business owners, an 'employee mindset' can be especially hard to shake. And it leads to exactly the scenario that Haami faced - working very hard to build a faster hamster wheel.

Why does this happen to so many business owners? Why do they work themselves into the ground, eventually either going bust, selling up, or giving up?

The answer lies in our past.

We're conditioned through our entire early lives to expect a near-immediate reward for nearly everything we do. In school, if we study hard and do well on tests, we'll get praise from our parents and maybe a place at university.

Then in our professional lives, if we work hard and for long hours, we'll get a bonus or promotion.

This traditional, transactional nature of work doesn't apply when you're a business owner. But it's often the hardest mindset shift to navigate. We think that because we're the boss, we should work the hardest. Do the most hours. Sacrifice the most. Whereas instead, we should be leveraging our resources (time, money, people) to get things done.

By the time we enter our first entrepreneurial endeavor, most of us have experienced decades of immediate reward for our efforts. But in business, the biggest payoffs often come from delayed gratification.

Delayed gratification can look like researching your market thoroughly before jumping in and making a fancy Clickfunnels sales page (only to find it doesn't convert because you didn't lay the groundwork).

It can look like holding off on that exciting new Facebook ad campaign until you're nailed your message-to-market match. Because jumping in before laying the foundations correctly costs you time and money. And you're not in business to waste those, are you?

Especially in the startup phase of business, when you're focused on making enough money to pay your bills and your staff, it can be hard to relate how creating your vision is going to actually help you.

So you write goals instead... but without a vision, you can't really anchor them to anything meaningful. (Why am I trying to get to 10 clients? What will that actually do for me?)

But If you don't define a clear vision of what you ultimately want, eventually you'll reach a glass ceiling and stagnate in your business. There will come a point where the money is no longer a strong motivator.

Or you'll reach a limitation in your mindset where you've reached a perceived limit of 'success' and there's nothing bigger to pull you further through the journey. Without a bigger challenge, the work loses its shine.

The transition from employee to business owner is a significant mindset shift, but it's a crucial one. Because there are going to be some things in your business that you can't see a specific financial reward for doing, but that doesn't mean they're not worth doing. In fact, quite the opposite.

Instead of a linear work = money perspective, as a business owner you need to think multi-dimensionally. You need to start recognizing that some things with no tangible value are actually the most important if you want to play the game of business at higher levels.

Your vision, mission, and values and goals are among those things.

That's why in the first few chapters of this book, you're going to create them. If you've already got them, you're going to revisit and refine them until they're pointy sharp.

Because your vision needs to be clear and actionable. It needs to live, breathe, and work. After all, it's got a big job to do. It needs to give you purpose beyond just running the hamster wheel with the illusion you're going somewhere.

Your plan to get off the hamster wheel

I get that creating your vision is not exactly #1 on your priority list. You're much more focused on making money, delivering a service, getting clients, and so on.

Maybe you intend to do it one day. But for the most part, business never slows down. Even in 'slow' periods, there's always a bunch of other things to do.

So you never get clear on <u>what you really want</u> from all this work you're doing.

Why am I actually building this business? What's the end goal?
As Haami puts it, "I was so busy doing the day-to-day, I never stepped away and asked myself 'what am I actually doing all this for?'"

Then a few years in, you're still working your guts out, searching for the pot at the end of the rainbow that is 'success'. More clients. More staff. More money. More problems... and the bigger the business gets, the more it consumes you.

Until one day you realize you don't want to do it anymore. You hate your business. You hate the demands it places on you. You are working more, and getting paid less than you were in your last job. You're hardly seeing your kids, and you're distracted when you do manage some 'quality' time with family.

You may even find yourself remembering your old life as an employee through rose-colored glasses as a fairyland of cushy offices, regular lunch breaks, a steady paycheck (even if you took time off!), and colleagues who didn't come to you with every damn issue.

The best part: the ultimate success or failure of the entire enterprise was *someone else's problem*.

Oh, things were so much easier then. Why did I go into business? What am I doing?
And so you either close the business or hand it over to someone else.

I don't want that for you.

So it's time to create your ultimate VISION.

Because when you know where you want to end up, you can organize your resources to get you there.

Most of us get into business to create a greater experience of life for ourselves. We want more choice, more financial freedom, more time doing the things we love.

Ultimately we go into business to create some form of desired state. A new way to live. A different, better way.

By the end of the chapter, you're going to feel connected with what you ultimately want from all this.

You're going to have the clarity to create a one-sentence vision for your business. I'll take you through the steps our The Opulence System™ members use to create visions that fuel their focus and energy through the good and not-so-good days.

If you already have a vision, I ask you to be willing to explore it a little deeper, change perspective, and perhaps even tweak it a little. Or maybe... just maybe, you'll decide to go in with a clean slate and see if your current vision is truly what you still want.

The vision you'll create in this chapter will underpin the work we're going to do throughout the rest of the book. It's the foundation for your goals, your company culture, your hiring policies, even your organizational structure.

Ultimately, your vision is your North Star. It will always light your way.

Before we get started, let's first get a greater understanding of what a vision is (and isn't), why it's important, how it fits into a broader strategy, and some common pitfalls to avoid when creating your own.

What a vision is (and isn't)

Your vision is your reason for doing what you do. Why are you getting up every day and going to work in your business? Why do you contribute in the way that you do? What's your driving force?

Behind your vision is your *desired state*. It's your WHY. It's that drive that underpins everything you do. Everything you spend your life moving towards trying to achieve. When you've got a strong enough 'why', the 'how' takes care of itself.

Your vision is not 'I want to make a million bucks a year'. That's a mission. I'll explain the difference between vision, mission, and values in a minute.

But first, let me make this clear -

Your vision is like the sunset. You never catch it. But it's beautiful enough that you keep striving for it.

Your mission (we'll cover more of this in Chapter 3) involves the big 10-year assignments or BHAGs (big hairy audacious goals) that will bring you closer to that sunset.

Your vision is what's left if you took away the money, the power... whatever reason you have for growing your business. If you took all the rewards away, your vision is the reason you still get out of bed. It's the thing that connects you to your purpose, beyond any material reward.

One last thing - your vision for your business is aligned with what you want personally. Otherwise, what's the point?

3 reasons your vision is critical for your success

For the skeptics feeling tempted to skip the 'fluffy stuff' and bypass this chapter... I hope you don't. Because a clear vision has some quietly powerful payoffs.

1. It fuels a positive emotional state
Running a business can sometimes feel like jumping out of a plane without a parachute. At some point, you're destined to hit the ground, hard.

As you go through the unavoidable ups and downs of business (and life), it helps to have a bigger purpose to keep going. Something to strive for that's greater than yourself.

For me personally, there have been many times in business where I thought about chucking it in. We're only human, and business can be challenging. We have crappy days. We get tired. We get disappointed. We get hurt by bad client feedback or problems with partners or staff.

But because my vision is so strong, it has always kept me focused on what my real goals are. Connecting with my vision on days I don't want to get out of bed gives me the spark I need to face the day in a positive state.

It will for you, too.

Besides, if you're not in business to fulfill a personal vision for your life, you may as well go get a job. Let someone else worry about capital growth and staff wages and every other damn thing.

But you don't want that. You want something more, don't you? Once you identify what that looks like, you can chart a path to get it.

2. It attracts A-player people

Great employees don't want a 'clock in, clock out' job where they're just a cog in a machine. They want to feel part of something greater than themselves. They want something to work towards that has a purpose aligned with their own personal values.

Good employees are looking to see if you're the type of leader who can do the hard work of thinking into the future. If you have a team of people and there's no vision for the future, it's near impossible to keep them engaged and motivated. And also harder to convince them to stick around.

The bottom line is your employees are directly responsible for the success of your business. And the quality of your people reflects the quality of your systems, your customer service, your efficiency, and every other aspect of your organization.

A clear vision doesn't just help attract top performers. It also helps motivate them to bring their best self to work. To dedicate their time, energy, creativity, and intelligence to help you make your vision a reality.

3. It promotes efficient decision making

In business, you'll face a lot of 'shiny objects' that lure you from your path. Sometimes several times a day!

Should I take that speaking opportunity? Do I need a shiny new sales funnel? Should I cut that underperforming service? Do I need a 14-day Clickfunnels trial? *Am I headed in the right direction?*

It's easy to wander down a tangent path and waste years (and thousands of dollars) only to realize it's not the right move for your business. Having a clear vision and mission is a yardstick that makes every business decision easy.

It also sets a broader strategic plan for your organization. It's very easy to get bogged down on the day-to-day details of running a business. Your vision statement helps you plan long-term.

Instead of getting confused and distracted when considering a new tactic or task, all you need to ask is: 'Is it aligned with our vision?' Then it's a simple yes or no.

Vision, mission, and values - what's the difference?

Think of a mountain. At the top of the mountain is a sunset (or sunrise, if you're an early bird). There's a path up the mountain. And signposts along the way.

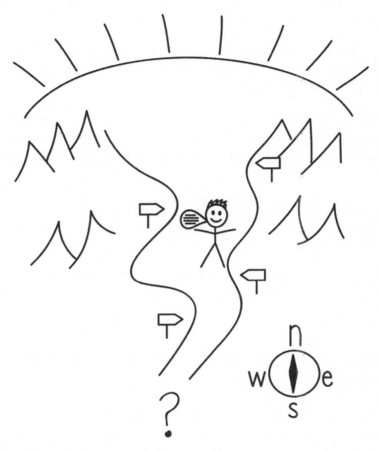

Your vision is the sunset over the mountain.

At The Game Changers, our vision is to help people activate their true potential and live a life beyond their wildest dreams.

If you think it sounds a bit cloudy, you're right. Your vision should be exciting enough that you're always striving for it, but abstract enough that you never 'finish' it.

Your mission is the road up the hill. It's the pathway that leads to your vision.

You can have any number of missions. They're the BHAGs (big hairy audacious goals) that are part of your 10-year plan.

For example, our mission at The Game Changers is to create an energized and opulent community of 1,000 conscious leaders by 2025 who are actively collaborating, contributing, and evolving through game-changing training and community activities.

It's a bit more tangible, isn't it? But still pretty big.

Your goals are the signposts along the way. They show you're on the right track, and help you keep moving towards your mission, which helps you move towards your vision.

Goals are what you end up with when you reverse-engineer your mission, and break it down into annual, quarterly, monthly, weekly and daily actionable chunks. (I'll show you how to do this effectively in Chapter 5).

Your values work as a compass that tells you whether you're moving in the right direction or not. Because without hiring to your values, operating in accordance with your values, bringing on clients that share your values and so on... you're going to encounter a lot more problems than you should.

Mapping your vision, mission, and goals means that if you just follow the plan, you will automatically move towards your vision.

At The Game Changers, the reason we've been able to help our clients achieve such rapid success (tripled profits and doubled time off in 12 months or less), is because of this high-level planning.

I was speaking with a mortgage broker client who has closed $20 million worth of deals in his last month - his biggest month ever by far - and he attributed it to the renewed focus he has thanks to our vision, mission, and goals model. It cuts out the noise and gives ultimate clarity on where you should be spending your time.

As for Haami, after going through this process he restructured his entire business around his vision. He's created his mission, goals, KPIs, org chart, team, and systems to all feed into it.

These days, instead of showing up at the worksite at 3.30am and having his day run him ragged, he and his team have structure, organization... and Haami actually loves being in business again!

"I've always had visions of where my business would be, but they were vague and not helpful. Going through this process has helped me sharpen my focus and really define what I'm doing all this for."

Before we dive into the process, let me give you a few quick tips for making sure your vision is as powerful as possible.

Vision as an avoidance strategy

Sometimes our vision can work really well if it's part of an avoidance strategy. As an example, let's look at Tony Robbins. When he started coaching, he did it to avoid the poverty he grew up with. As a child, money was always out of reach for Tony, and therefore a source of stress. There was never enough of it. That experience fuelled his vision of what he wanted his life to look like.

Perhaps you've had a similar experience.

In fact, the majority of people in this world are more focused on avoiding pain than moving towards pleasure.

I don't want to struggle for money,

I don't want to live the way my parents lived,

I don't want to experience insecurity,

I don't want to be lonely,

I don't want to worry about ......

You don't have to look too far for your vision. It's related to you, after all.

What were the experiences you had growing up, or even 5, 6 years ago? Often our 'why' is something inside of us that wants to overcome the experiences we once had, or to make sure others don't go through that same experience.

So when you start creating your vision (there's a worksheet at the end of this chapter), if you can't think of what you DO want... start with what you DON'T want. That can be just as useful.

Common traps to avoid when creating your vision

The money trap

As you're reading this, it's quite possible that your vision is centered around making more money. Or to get a greater amount of time freedom.

In the beginning, it's easy to say 'I want to make a million bucks a year', or another arbitrary amount you think will make you feel successful.

But money is not anything in itself - it's just a tool. What we really want is a *feeling*.

We want the feeling of being able to pay for dinner with friends without checking our bank account. We want the feeling that being able to provide for our family and take them on nice holidays brings. We want the feeling that contributing to our community brings.

Money is just the vehicle to get us to our desired state. And if we focus our vision solely around money, we'll never reach that goal. Because the only thing you want when you get money is more money. That's not a fun sunset to gaze at!

So be aware that money and time are GOALS... they're not a vision. *Why* do you want time and money? What will it give you? What will you do once you have them? Without having a vision, you'll probably get kind of lost...

Think of the lotto winners who blow their entire prize within 5 years. Think of the retirees whose physical and mental health decline rapidly when they suddenly have all this time... but nothing to do.

Money and time are short term acquisitions - not a long-term legacy.

The perfection trap

Some business owners spend months agonizing over nailing their 'perfect' vision.

Don't spend too much time trying to get it right. Your vision, mission, and values are all something that you'll keep cultivating as you journey through growing your business (and your next, and the next, if you choose to do so).

If you are just starting out and don't really have a strong vision for what you want, that is ok. It will develop as you progress. And as Haami found when he went through this exercise, the more you look into it, the more you'll discover about yourself.

So don't get obsessed with getting it 'right'. There is no 'perfect'. In fact, your vision will change and evolve over time, as you yourself change and evolve. It's not set in stone, unchangeable forever. It's part of you.

Just focus on getting enough clarity over your vision that you can see a short distance forward.

Think of driving a car at night… the headlights don't illuminate your entire journey at once, do they? They simply light up the path that's in front of you.

The show-off trap

Your vision doesn't have to be some grandiose plan to feed 50 million people and change the world forever. It doesn't have to be some large scale global dream.

This is where many people get it wrong. They think of their vision in terms of what others might think of it. Or they look at someone else's vision and think, 'that's great, I'll adopt that for myself'.

Your vision must start with YOU. If it's not an expression of your true desires, you're not going to align with it. It's not going to fuel you or inspire you. It won't give you the buzz needed to get through the day when things get tough.

Your vision doesn't need to change the world. It can just be enough to change YOUR world.

Especially in your first few years in business, you can - and probably should - just start off with something as simple as -

'I want to create a business that lets me be there for my kids for school pick-ups and drop-offs, and when they need me'.
or;

'I want to create a business that puts enough money in my pocket that I can shout my friends to dinner whenever I want without having to check my bank balance first or eat 2-minute noodles for the rest of the week.'

Especially when you're in the startup phase of your business, you're very much fighting for survival. You're trying to pay staff and attract clients and generate cash-flow.

So you cannot be thinking of contribution on a greater scale yet. You cannot be thinking globally when you're struggling to turn a consistent profit from month to month. Your business just isn't there yet. And that's perfectly OK.

So instead, think of a vision that is relevant to where you are NOW.

When your business is systemized to work without you, and you're making consistent profits, and you've got a great team in place, *then* you can start thinking about contributing on a wider scale.

But you've gotta take care of yourself first. What do airlines instruct you to do during an in-flight emergency? Put your oxygen mask on first, before helping others.

Let's do this

Now you've got a greater understanding of what a vision is (and isn't), why it's important, how it fits into a broader strategy and common pitfalls to avoid.

It's time to put your knowledge to work.

Some of the questions you're about to read look the same. But they have been languaged slightly differently for a reason. We're using a framework from Neuro-Linguistic Programming (NLP) that's designed to help you connect to your deeper desired state - what's *really* going on in your heart.

Imagine that right now I've just placed a magic wand in your hands. And there are no limitations on money, on time, on location… you have that magic wand and you can wave it now.

Get rid of the 'shoulds' and 'coulds'… give yourself permission to dream. There are no limitations right now, except the ones you place on yourself.

Wave your wand. Dream. Write down whatever comes to mind. Don't censor it. There are no rights or wrongs. Anything is possible.

PART A: DREAM

1. What would you like?

2. What would you want?

3. If you had that, what would that do for you?

Feel into this one. What would you experience, feel, behave like?

4. And if you had that? What would that do for you?

Keep asking yourself this question until you can no longer think or feel anything else. Every time you answer this question, think: 'For what purpose'? Dig down deeper with each time you ask this question, get through the surface stuff and connect with your subconscious mind.

5. How would you know if you had that?

What are the experiences, things, feelings, people that would indicate to you that you had what you wanted? We chase these materialistic things, but what we really want is the feeling we'll have when we have them. We don't want the car - we want the feeling of driving it (and seeing our neighbors envy)…

6. What are you most excited about right now or in the coming years?

What are the people, the surroundings, the events?

7. What are your big opportunities in the next year?

If anything was possible, what would that look like for you?

8. Fast forward 1, 3 or 5 years from now and you were a fly on the wall and the people you respected were talking about you, what would you be hearing them say about what you are doing, or what you've been up to?

9. Why does anyone care about what you do?

10. How do the people working in your business feel about it?

)If it's just yourself, how do you feel about it?) If you interviewed them, what would they say?

11. What are 3 things you are proud of 1 year from now?

12. What are 3 things you are proud of 3 years from now?

13. This next year will be a year that...... (what happens)?

14. Are there any new relationships you want to establish this year?

Think new mentors, new friends, new team members

PART B: CREATE

The next part is to create a story that captures as much of your dreams as you can. If life was exactly how you wanted it to be, and you're journalling right now on this perfect day in your perfect life… what does it look like? Write it like a mini-story.

Now, this is a start - the key is to get it down to one sentence, but having that story - helps to get to the bottom of what it is you ultimately want to create.

When you have your mini-story, drill down to its essence until you have ONE sentence that captures what you essentially want to achieve.

For example, The Game Changers' vision is: 'To activate every being's truest potential and experience life beyond their wildest dreams'

What will yours be?

Now put down this book and spend 20-30minutes on the exercise. Download a worksheet from our website at www.pathtofreedom.com.au/resources

Because remember that knowledge is useless without IMPLEMENTING that knowledge. So take action. Then move to the next chapter. I'll be waiting.

YOUR MISSION

YOUR MISSION

"Having a mission means that instead of spending our day putting out spot-fires, we focus our time on high-level activities that get us to where we ultimately want to be."

Vanessa Fiducia & Edie May
Profit First Accounting

Vanessa's eyes well up with tears. She has to look away.

It's 2019 and we're chatting at The Game Changers quarterly Business Intensive event in Perth, Australia. I've taken Vanessa and Edie aside to record a quick testimonial video during a break.

Although the sun is shining, the mood momentarily gets gloomy. What had I said to elicit such an unexpectedly emotional response? I'd just asked them what life was like 9 months ago...

As Vanessa composes herself, her business partner Edie steps in. "You have to understand Barry, Vanessa was working 90 hour weeks. She slept at the office most week nights. Every tax season, she'd hardly see her kids for three months. And for all this we were just scraping by, paying ourselves $200 a week."

"It sounds absolutely awful. You weren't in control of your business," I said.

"Barry, we were barely in control of ourselves," Edie replied. "Clients would drop off work at my house at 7am on Sunday morning. They'd call us at 1am to ask a question. Whatever they wanted, they got. When they said jump, we said how high."

Vanessa's intention behind her 90 hour weeks was pure. But it followed the flawed logic of the 'employee mindset' I spoke about in the introduction of this book. She figured if she worked hard to build the business up, eventually it would give her the freedom to spend more time with her family. Hard work equals reward, right?

But the hard work just led to more hard work.

I know the problem well, having experienced it myself in my first cabinetry business, and seeing it in new clients when they join The Opulence System™. We get so excited about running our new business, and so determined to make it work, that we take on a lot of things we shouldn't.

Especially clients.

This might sound counter-intuitive. But the thing is, although clients equal money, the wrong ones cost you enormously. In fact, the wrong clients will actually drag your business backwards.

Taking on every client, and doing all of the work yourself (instead of leveraging your resources to get it done for you), won't get you where you want to go. It will just max out your time, energy, and your money. Just like Vanessa and Edie, you end up working ridiculous hours yet getting paid peanuts!

Your mission helps safeguard your business against unsuitable clients and other resource-wasting activities. It keeps your business on track to achieve your ultimate vision. It's your path to the sunset.

As Edie puts it, "Nine months ago, our mindset was that we needed every client. We took on everyone and broke our backs for them. Now we have our vision and mission, we carefully vet potential clients to ensure that if we take them on, we're both going to move forward in the direction we want to go."

Vanessa nods in agreement. Nine months prior, she was often tired and snapped at her staff, her partner, and her kids. She resented the business, because it took everything from her without giving anything back.

She felt that everything relied on her. If it didn't get done, she had to do it. And she had to get everything right too. That's an enormous amount of pressure!

"Now I get texts from my staff thanking me for being such a great boss, and telling me they love their job," Vanessa beams. "That's happening because now I'm feeling in control, for the first time in a long time. I'm calm. I enjoy the business again. Because I know where we're going, and we're making real progress in getting there."

If you're experiencing something similar to Vanessa and Edie's previous predicament in your own business, in this chapter you're going to take the first step in fixing it. And if you haven't experienced it yet, let's make sure you never do.

Defining your mission is the second of three foundational elements (vision, mission, values) of a systemized and scalable business that aligns your lifestyle with your truest desires. It's the first step in reverse-engineering a path to your ultimate vision.

Later on, you'll turn your mission into practical, actionable goals that lead the way. But for now, we need to define what your mission is.

If your vision is the WHY...

Your mission is the WHAT.

(Your values are the HOW. We'll get to these in the next chapter.)

HOW THIS STARTS TO PIECE TOGETHER....

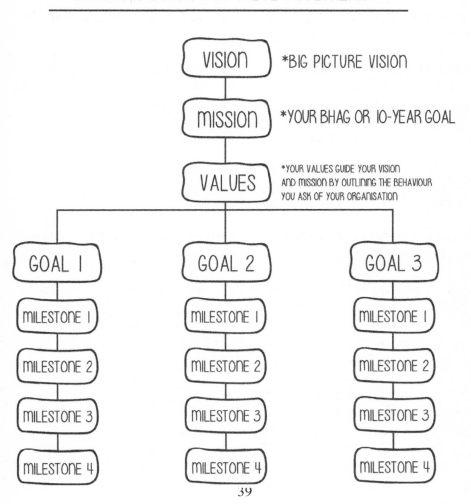

VISION — *BIG PICTURE VISION

MISSION — *YOUR BHAG OR 10-YEAR GOAL

VALUES — *YOUR VALUES GUIDE YOUR VISION AND MISSION BY OUTLINING THE BEHAVIOUR YOU ASK OF YOUR ORGANISATION

GOAL 1 — MILESTONE 1 — MILESTONE 2 — MILESTONE 3 — MILESTONE 4

GOAL 2 — MILESTONE 1 — MILESTONE 2 — MILESTONE 3 — MILESTONE 4

GOAL 3 — MILESTONE 1 — MILESTONE 2 — MILESTONE 3 — MILESTONE 4

As you've probably figured out by now, setting your vision, mission and values aren't woo-woo exercises that serve to just look good on a wall. They're the first steps in the strategic planning required for creating a business that fuels your ultimate lifestyle (instead of sucking you dry).

This is why this 3 step foundational process I'm taking you through in these first chapters is so important for the growth you're going to achieve after you implement all steps on the path to freedom.

I could have just written a book on sales or marketing, and sold a heap of copies promising 'ninja hacks' and 'hidden tricks' and whatever else. But the results you'd get wouldn't be as sustainable or long-term without building this solid business foundation first.

Creating your vision, mission and values may not provide the instant gratification of launching a shiny new sales funnel or Facebook ad campaign, but they are the true power of this structure.

They're the key for unlocking extraordinary growth in your business - and rapidly too.

Your first steps

By now you should have completed your vision statement. If not, go and do it now before proceeding.

These steps in the path to freedom are designed so that each step layers upon the last. If you don't know what your vision, mission, and values are, the rest of the process won't work. Because you won't have defined exactly what you're building. In construction, building without a plan leads to disaster. It's the same in business.

By the end of this chapter, you'll know how you're going to actively move towards achieving your vision. You'll have 1 or 2 'big hairy audacious goals' (BHAGS) that will light the path of your business journey for the next 10 years.

Don't be put off by the enormity of this - we'll be breaking your mission down into manageable quarterly, monthly, weekly and daily goals in Chapter 5. So it's important that you don't skip past this chapter. Because as with everything in life, you can't get the results you want without doing the work required.

Looking through the gym window and planning to jump on the treadmill later won't shed those kilos. Likewise, reading this book and planning to take action later won't help you create a business that gives you the freedom to do whatever you please.

If you have completed your vision statement, congratulations. I'm sure that you're now much clearer on what you actually want from your business, and where you're moving towards. You've sketched your sunset.

Now let's put some real-life actionables in place to help you move towards it and fulfill your dreams.

Your path up the mountain

Remember the picture of the sunset from the last chapter?

Here it is again:

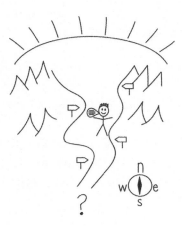

Your mission is the path leading up the mountain. It's a massive 10-year goal that will bring you closer to your vision.

For example:

Vision = End world hunger

Mission = Feed 100,000 families in a 3rd world country by the end of 2030

Your mission specifies exactly who you're going to help, and how you're going to help them. A great mission statement communicates:

1. the markets you're going to serve,

2. the benefits you're going to offer,

3. the problems you're going to solve,

4. the solutions you're providing,

Think of a GPS. If you put an address into the GPS in your car, it will give you a few options for different routes to get there. All suggested routes will get you to your destination, but some are shorter. Some are more scenic. Some have lots of turns and traffic lights.

Your mission is kind of like your business GPS. It maps out the path you will take to get to the vision you wish to create.

For example, our mission at The Game Changers is To create an energised and opulent community of 1,000 conscious leaders by 2025 who are actively collaborating, contributing, and evolving through game changing training, and community activities.

The Opulence System™ is the vehicle through which we execute this mission. And when we're on mission, we know we're on track to fulfill our vision: '*To activate every being's truest potential and experience life beyond their wildest dreams*'.

Think of it like this: your mission is a high-level plan for producing a

tangible result that's aligned with your vision.

Challenges you'll encounter without a mission

Without a mission, there's nothing in place to actually make your vision happen. It's just a dream, and will always remain so. And what's the point of working if you're not fulfilling your ultimate purpose?

Vanessa and Edie found that out the hard way. Their life was work, stress and pressure from the wrong places (and people).

Running a business without a clear mission means you'll also encounter a few other unwelcome challenges. Perhaps you're dealing with some of these now?

Procrastination and lack of motivation

While being unclear on your vision creates a lack of drive, being unclear on your mission creates procrastination.

Have you ever avoided doing a task because you knew it was going to take a lot of mental energy to figure out? Or because it just seemed so enormous to tackle that you felt tired just thinking of it?

Procrastination comes from uncertainty. When we're not sure of exactly what to do, we hesitate. Having a mission gets you clear on what you're doing and motivated to do it.

Playing the game of business with no desire to win

Without a mission to bring you closer to your vision, you're really just working for the sake of it. Your business keeps you busy, but with no clear direction, and what's worse, no emotional reward. You're running on a hamster wheel, without a plan to get off the damn thing. In short: you've got a job.

When you're not sure exactly what goals, tasks, or priorities are going to get you closer to your vision, everything is just stuff to do. There's no clear path. It's just a jumbled mess. How utterly depressing!

No wonder business owners without a clear vision, mission, and goals end up trapped by their own creation.

Scattered focus

If your vision is to create a lifestyle business for yourself where you're only working one or two hours a week, you wouldn't want to embark on a mission of opening 100 retail stores in Australia. Or a mission to sign 10 clients for 1:1 work. Or anything else that is clearly not going to help you achieve that lifestyle you're after.

Think of our GPS analogy. Without a defined path, you'd be driving around for hours trying to find your address by trial and error. What an enormous waste of time and energy (and petrol).

Your mission draws the line in the sand between what you want and most importantly, what you *don't* want. Shiny objects that try and distract you are easy to avoid when you have a plan in place for achieving your vision. With a mission, you have a strong focus and a straighter path.

Not thinking big enough

I don't mean you should necessarily have plans for world domination. You don't have to aspire to be the next Elon Musk or Jeff Bezos.

By thinking big I mean getting really excited about the possibilities for your business and your life.

Not long ago, Edie told me, "Vanessa percolates every night. Every morning she calls me full of energy and new ideas for where we can take our business. That didn't happen before. We were so overworked that we didn't have the time or headspace to think of anything except the work that was right in front of us."

Look, there are actually very few rules in life. There are the obvious moral and societal ones (don't kill, steal or otherwise behave like a douchebag) but other than that, there are actually no rules on how to live. Only the rules we make for ourselves.

This is where we imprison ourselves: we create our rules based on what we *think* we should want. Or based on what others expect from us. Or we seek to emulate our neighbour Joe because he seems really successful. Then we wonder why we feel so unfulfilled.

When we live with no connection to what our heart is telling us, it's a road to misery.

And besides, you're an entrepreneur. A rebel of sorts. You don't want to work 50 years for the proverbial gold watch and quiet retirement, do you? You want to do things differently, right?

So *think* differently.

Just because you're running a business doesn't mean you have to sit at a desk for 40 hours a week. It doesn't mean that you have to run your business like the others in your industry do. It doesn't mean that you have to follow the path your parents want for you. Or society. Or whatever.

The fact is life can be as wonderful as we want to make it. Or as limiting. It all comes back to your mindset: what do you unconsciously believe you are capable of achieving? What do you unconsciously believe that you deserve to get?

Challenge the 'rules' you have made for yourself. Question where they came from, and if they are what your heart really wants.

Your limiting beliefs are like shadows - you don't notice they are there until you shine a light on them. When you see them clearly, they have less power over you. You can begin to change them to new empowering beliefs.

When you make your own rules, you can achieve anything.

Elon Musk dreams up unconventional business ideas that 99.999% of the population would never even consider as remotely possible. He's currently building underground Hyperloop transportation tunnels under several cities, merging human brains with computers at Neuralink, and is aiming to provide enough solar energy to power the planet with his SolarCity project.

He also once sold $10 million worth of gas torches by marketing them as flamethrowers to ward off the zombie apocalypse. Oh, and he's about to spearhead space tourism with his company SpaceX. And he wants to colonize Mars.

Radical ideas? Yes. Will he achieve them anyway? Most of them probably.

The lesson here is this:

You may not be Elon Musk. But you can still achieve whatever you put your damn mind to. So make it something that excites the hell out of you. Throw out the rules. Dream big.

Defining your mission

It's time to start thinking about YOUR mission.

What does your business need to do to give you the experience you wish to create?

Remember my GPS analogy from earlier. It's important that you define the route you're going to take up the mountain. Or you could end up anywhere. Or nowhere.

Let's look at Disney's mission statement:

"To be one of the world's leading producers and providers of entertainment and information, using our portfolio of brands to differentiate our content, services and entertainment experiences and related products in the world."

Yes, it's a mouthful. But it's also specific on what they're doing, who they're doing it for and how they're doing it.

Disney's clear vision and mission are the backbone of the company. They're the reason Disney is still a leader of the pack today, nearly 100 years after its humble beginnings in a small shared office in Los Angeles.

So what is *your* mission

Again, this still might be a work in progress. You might have begun to get clear on your mission as you've read this chapter. Or you might need to pull together a few tiny threads and start there.

Either way, it's perfectly ok.

What's more important is that you take action. Imperfect action is far better than no action at all. (Besides, perfection is unachievable. If you constantly aim for 'perfect', stop doing that.)

These first few chapters are dedicated to layering the structure and foundation that you need to create to build a profitable, predictable and purposeful business that works without you.

Setting your mission is kind of like stepping up to the starting blocks... things start moving really fast over what's coming next.

Let's do this

Similar to creating your vision, creating your mission is divided into 2 parts: Dreaming and Creating.

Let's jump into the dream space first. Remember, anything is possible here. There are no rules on what you can and cannot do. Tell the primal critter in your brain to shush and let you exist in a creative space for a while.

There are no limitations. Write like crazy. Don't self-edit.

And ponder...

PART A: DREAM

1. What are your 10-year goals?

I like to think of a vision as a 100-year goal. It's a bit bigger than what we can ever fully achieve. Your mission is what breaks down your path to this vision into 10-year blocks or BHAGs (big hairy audacious goals). Write at least 10 of these. Just let your mind go wild.

2. What is the service or product you're providing?

Are you a service-based business? Or do you sell products? Do you sell B2B or B2C? Get specific.

This might seem obvious. "I sell garden equipment Barry. What more do you want me to say?" But this is an opportunity to question whether you're providing the right service or product. Is it aligned with your vision? Or does it need a tweak?

There's no golden rule saying that you should keep selling what you started out selling. In fact, quite the opposite - pivoting and reimagining your service offer to align more closely with your vision is a good thing. For you and for your clients.

3. How do you do it?

How do you provide your product or service? Get specific.

4. What market do you wish to serve?

Note that this question is NOT asking 'who do I currently serve'... Instead, I want you to think 'who do I *want* to serve? Who do I enjoy working with? What type of people can I give the most value to?'

5. What is the value or benefit you wish to provide?

You might already be providing this, or it might be an extension of where you want to take your business long-term. If you could provide any value, what would it be? The more it aligns with your personal values, the stronger your mission will become.

That's it for the questions.

Now comes the creation side of the exercise.

PART B: CREATE

Once you've answered the first 5 dream-space questions, summarise it into a mission statement for your business. Remember to be specific about WHO you serve, WHAT you do, and HOW you do it.

Tip: don't write just one mission statement. Tweak and revise until you're comfortable with them. Then pick your favorite one - that's where we're going to start.

As with your vision statement, we've created a worksheet you can use. Download it for free at www.pathtofreedom.com.au/resources

Don't skip this - your mission is an important step on your path to freedom.

On our last call, Vanessa told me a beautiful story. She said, "Yesterday my kids came to the office to visit me, and we had an impromptu 4pm cake party. We sat and watched Netflix on the boardroom TV and drank tea and ate cake together."

"Sounds like a lovely way to spend an afternoon," I laughed.

"It was! That never would have happened before we aligned our business behind our mission," Vanessa continued. "But now I can do those kinds of things. I can step out of the business, know that my staff are getting the work done, and enjoy special time with my kids."

Freedom isn't running away and taking no responsibility for your business (or your life)... freedom is being able to do things like that because your life has balance.

Go and take action on this now. Put the book down, visit www.pathtofreedom.com.au/resources, and download your worksheet. Then take 30 minutes to do a little dreaming.

Don't let this book be another one on the shelf that you read but didn't take action on. Whatever other shiny object that's trying to get your attention right now, it's not going to get you any closer to your goal.

Time will pass either way. What will you do with it?

CASE STUDY

The Wealth Mentor

When mortgage broker Jackson first started with us, his business was successful but it felt like a lot of work. He and his 2 co-managers were often butting heads around what they considered the priorities of the business to be. Making decisions was a slow and painful process as it was difficult getting all 3 managers on board. In short: with no common vision to align behind, every day was a game of tug-of-war.

Despite this, Jackson and his team had scaled the branch very quickly. But they were too busy, and working on too many things without clear direction on how to continue that sustained growth.

Their scattered approach resulted in a lot of wasted time and opportunities. Despite working hard, the firm had hit a glass ceiling in terms of profits and output.

Within 9 months using The Opulence System™ (of which these 9 Steps are a part), Jackson quadrupled his revenue and topped the leaderboard of all brokerages in his state.

At the time of recording his case study, his team has closed $20 million worth of deals in his last month - his biggest month ever by far. And it's only the beginning…

Most importantly, despite the increase in profits, time spent at the office has actually decreased. Jackson has been able to step out of his business more to focus on high level planning to ensure he continues to lead his business from strength to strength.

Jackson attributes this success to the renewed focus he has thanks to our vision, mission, values and goals model. It cuts out the noise and gave Jackson and the team ultimate clarity on where they should be spending their time.

Decision making is easy, as all 3 managers are focused on the branch's goals, not their own personal goals. It's a simple matter of asking 'is this aligned with our vision, mission and goals?'. Personalities aside, it's the line in the sand.

Additionally, recruiting and retaining A-player staff is easy now there's well-defined goals and values for the business. It makes underperforming staff a thing of the past, and gives everyone a benchmark for measuring their own performance.

Having a clear vision, mission and goals also brought the branch's people together in an unexpected way. It transformed them from a group of individual brokers all working to achieve more money for themselves personally (and butting heads daily along the way), into a cohesive team all working towards the same vision for the business.

Now going to work is an exciting and positive experience. Instead of constant friction between brokers, there's co-operation, accountability, drive, and a genuine enjoyment of the job.

When you align your team behind a vision everyone can get excited about, work is easier, more rewarding and far more profitable.

Watch   Jackson's   case   study   here   ->
https://www.thegamechangers.com.au/jackson-millan-wealth-mentor/

YOUR VALUES

YOUR VALUES

"Creating my business values was always on the backburner, but it never seemed urgent. But looking back, now I know that everything in my business links back to them."

Matt Boyd, Bathurst Automotive

It's Wednesday at 8pm on a balmy Bali day.

After finishing a healthy dinner, I log into my private coaching group on Facebook to see how everyone's going.

A relatively new member, Matt, has just posted an update -

Hi everyone, just wanted to share this quick note. For ages we have had a toxic person in our business, and we finally ended his employment with us.

We dragged it out so long hoping he'd change which never really happened. From time to time he was good but for the most he was abusing the system.

It's amazing how much stress has lifted off my shoulders. Now I can concentrate on my business and my family.

It's also amazing how much better the team is going. Like me, they have been stressed over this person and since he's left the whole team has jumped into another gear and are working so well together. Things are getting done on time and they are all going above and beyond expectations.

We now have a great team that works together. It's great to have a family at work as well.

YES, MATT!!

I feel like driving the 3,733 kilometers from Perth to Bathurst just to give him a massive high-five. I watched Matt struggle with the decision to let this employee go for 2 months. And he'd finally made the decision to value himself, and his team, over one staff member.

Matt runs an automotive services business in a small town about two hours north-west of Sydney.

He's a softly spoken guy. He's not the type of person who is comfortable bulldozing his team into line. Like many business owners, Matt established his business through the love of his craft - auto mechanics. Back in our very first meeting, he confessed to me that he's not 'a business person'.

Despite this perceived limitation, Matt's business took off, and soon he was managing a team of 8 mechanics. He hired new mechanics purely on experience. After all, that was the only yardstick he had to go by.

Not surprisingly, as the team grew, the cracks started to show…

Matt had hired one person in particular who looked great on paper, but wasn't the right fit for the business. The guy was often late to work. He was argumentative. He wasn't interested in helping others on his team. The working relationship soon turned toxic.

In every conversation Matt had with this staff member, he found himself railroaded by the guy's steadfast refusal to do things a different way. He thought he knew better than Matt, and that was that.

In one of our early coaching sessions, I told Matt, "Until you create a set of business values, you'll have no guidelines for the type of people you want working in the business, or the standards you want them to meet."

Shortly after, Matt implemented a set of company-wide values designed to establish a clear standard in terms of both work quality and attitude.

Most of his staff welcomed the changes, and were enthusiastic about 'the new normal'.

That is, except for that one toxic staff member.

"He just wouldn't fall into line. No matter how I treated him, no matter how much everyone else in the team was on board with the business values, he still resisted. I eventually realised that he wasn't going to change. He thought he was above the rules and didn't want to contribute as part of the team."

Matt had a feeling before that he wasn't the right fit for the business, but he was reluctant to let him go because of the experience he brought to the role. But after establishing his business values, Matt saw just how misaligned this hire was.

"I constantly butted heads with my toxic employee. My team were like kids watching their parents argue - it was stressful for everyone and caused fractured focus and lost productivity."

But still Matt hesitated.

"I thought letting this guy go was going to leave a huge hole in my business."

Matt had to make a choice - was he going to let this guy hold his business hostage? Or was he going to place his business' value, and his team's value, above this one person?

When he finally 'ripped off the bandaid' and parted ways with his unsuitable hire, the effect on the rest of the team was immediate.

"When I finally let him go, it was like the rest of the guys finally breathed out," Matt told me later. "It was like a weight was lifted off their shoulders. They all elevated their performance to match our values and things took off. I haven't even had to rehire for the role - we're doing 20% more revenue with one less staff member."

I wasn't surprised.

So often I meet business owners who believe that good staff are hard to find.

But that's simply not true.

There are plenty of creative, intelligent, driven and hard-working people out there. So why is recruiting such a nightmare for many business owners? Why is finding people who actually want to work like finding diamonds in a coal pit?

If you're currently having issues with staff, I'd wager it's because your vision, mission, and values either aren't strong enough, or your staff don't know they exist.

This chapter on values is the last foundational piece we're going to lay before we get into some hardcore business planning.

Remember that mountain picture from Chapter 2? Your vision was the sunset, and your mission was the path up the mountain. <u>Your values are the compass that keep you on that path.</u>

If your vision is the **why**, and your mission is the **how**, your values are the **what**.

How will you operate as a business, both externally and internally?

How will your organization treat its clients, peers, and staff?

Which guiding principles will underpin everything you do?

Your business values dictate the behaviors, actions, and decisions that shape your organization, every day.

You'll see in later chapters around hiring and managing your A-player team that values are the most important factor in building a high-performing and dedicated team who run your business for you.

For now, understand that values send a distinct message to the outside world about how you run your business. But most importantly, your values determine your culture *within* the business.

And a thriving business culture with strong values is what aligns your team, inspires them to bring their best to their role every day, and attracts the cream of the crop when hiring new staff.

But that's just the beginning…

Your values are your boundaries

I meet a lot of business owners who don't have clear boundaries within their business. They'll take on anything and everything to get up and running. They take on clients that aren't a good fit because they need the money. They hire staff that don't fit their culture (if there is one) because they need more hands-on-deck.

Then they get stuck on a hamster wheel because all of a sudden they've got a group of employees to look after. But the whole time they're not valuing themselves enough to say what they will (and will not) do.

So their clients run rings around them. Their staff take advantage of them. They spend each day getting the proverbial crap kicked out of them, one way or the other. But they're supposed to be the one calling the shots!

In short, they end up like Matt - getting held hostage by one team member who is holding the rest of the pack back.

Identifying your values helps you understand how you want to interact with the world around you.

How do you want to interact with your clients and customers?

How do you want to interact with your peers?

How do you want to interact with your staff?

Your values affect *everything* you do in business.

They affect hiring the right staff. Bringing on board the right clients. Making decisions within your business.

Case in point -

We've got a new member in The Opulence System™ who is going through the consequences of not hiring to his values right now.

His name is Tim.

Tim is in a similar position that Matt was in a couple of months ago.

He has an employee that's been with the business for years. He knows his way around and is a 'good' worker. But he directly works against the new culture that Tim is trying to create. He liked things the way they were before, and doesn't want to embrace Tim's new vision, mission, and values.

So this guy has to go, right? Because the longer he stays, the more he'll hurt the business with his attitude. At worst, he'll create a kind of rot that can creep from employee to employee, turning once-enthusiastic team members sour.

Despite this, Tim is afraid to let him go. Because he's operating from a place of scarcity. "I'm not going to find another guy who is as good."

This thinking basically screws business owners because they're afraid to let someone go because they're 'good', even though they don't fit in with the company culture.

But this fear can bring your whole organization down if you let it rule you. Let me tell you why.

Teaching others how to treat you

If you don't define how you want to be treated, others will do it for you.

In business, letting others define how you operate is a slippery slope to overwhelm, overwork, and often bankruptcy.

Through our own behaviour, we are constantly teaching others how to treat us. As the leader in your business, it's your job to be a living example of the standards you expect your team to meet.

It's easy to let things slip.

But know this:

>> If you answer client calls on weekends, you're telling them it's ok to call you after hours. You're telling them your personal time is not as important as their immediate need.

>> If you let your staff come in consistently late, you're telling them it's ok not to value your time.

>> If you let your sales team sign clients that aren't right for the business, you're telling them you care more about money than quality. And that it's ok for them to behave that way too.

>> If you let clients dictate the terms of your projects, you're telling them that you don't value your worth highly. It also signals that you are under-confident (and perhaps even underqualified).

The worst part - not only are you telling your team, your clients, and whoever else that it's ok to stomp on you... you're telling *yourself* that it's ok too. Just think about what this does to your self-esteem!

The values we choose to uphold don't only form our boundaries. They form our *standards*.

If we're willing to compromise on our standards, we're actually saying to everyone around us that it's ok for them to do so too.

Sweeping your values under the rug basically means you're saying to our staff that it's ok to not operate at the standard you say you want from them. That it's ok to not operate loyally. Or respectfully. Or with integrity. Or whatever it is that you hold important.

The power of 'NO'

We're taught from an early age that 'no' is a rude word. From toddlers, all through teenagehood, adults would scowl and berate us for simply trying to assert our boundaries.

While it is obviously important that young people learn that throwing food and chucking tantrums is not a great way to function in society, our conditioning against the word 'no' actually works against us in adulthood.

Because we're practically afraid to say no. We don't want to offend. Or upset. Or insult. We don't want to put someone else out. But asserting boundaries is essential for healthy adult functioning.

When we constantly say 'yes' to everything, it's exhausting. It's confusing (because you're not focused on your vision and mission - personal or otherwise). And it leads to resentment.

On a personal level, it can mean resenting that friend who is a 'taker' (even though you have positioned yourself as a giver). In business, it can mean resenting clients, resenting the projects you take on, and even resenting your business.

We often are more focused on holding on to what we have, then letting go so a new opportunity can come in.

Back to Tim's story from before, he eventually did let that toxic employee go. And just like Matt, when he did, not only did the rest of his team improve, but new hires came along who were a far better fit for the business.

<u>When you say no to what's not a fit, you make room for new things that are.</u>

When Tim decided to take action on what he wanted and what he valued, he drew the line in the sand. He set the standard for what he would - and wouldn't - accept in his business.

When we start saying 'no' to things that aren't aligned with our values... something wonderful happens. We actually begin to attract things that are aligned with who we are, and the values we uphold.

Let me get metaphysical with you for a minute...

The universe gives us what we ask for

Whether you believe in the Law of Attraction or not, you cannot deny that energy is everywhere. Our bodies are energy sources. Plants emit energy. Waves in the sea emit energy.

In fact, everything in our entire existence is part of the electromagnetic force, which is one of the four fundamental forces in nature (gravity, the weak nuclear force, the electromagnetic force, and the strong nuclear force).

Everything in our universe is electrically charged - right down to teeny atoms, photons, quarks and many other building blocks that exist within us and everything else.

So it stands to reason then, that given this electrical force running within everything, that energies have relationships with each other. At its most simple explanation, like the plus and minus ends of a battery, all energy attracts (or repels) other energy.

Given we've agreed on that (I'm assuming we have), let us also agree that the energy we put out into the universe has an effect.

In short, <u>the energy we project influences what we get back.</u>

Which is why when we start saying 'no', asserting boundaries, and living by our values, things start to show up that are in alignment with that energetic track.

Think of it as having tuned in to a new radio station. When you're living in congruence with your values, you're officially on YouFM. The signal is clear.

Now, that's not to say that if you just wish for a Lamborghini it will show up in your driveway tomorrow.

But when you're clear on your values, and live by them (cutting out the stuff that doesn't fit), you'll start to see the opportunities the Universe is putting in front of you.

If I'm getting too 'woo-woo' for you, consider this:

Have you ever decided to buy a car, and then started to see it on the road everywhere? I did this with my first car, a white Datsun Ute. After I bought it, they were absolutely everywhere. How had I not seen this before?

The truth is the Datsun Utes were always on the road. I just didn't see them until I focused my intention on buying one.

Where our focus goes, our energy flows and our results show.

Your values = your business DNA

Let's think back to earlier in this book where we talked about the ultimate goal: to create a business that's profitable and sustainable and works without you. Not necessarily because we don't want to be there, but because otherwise we just have a job.

To create that business, we need to create culture. Your culture is like the genetic code of your business. It cannot be bought or shipped in from somewhere. However, if you don't have a values alignment within your company, the culture can easily be torn down.

The best way to start building that culture is to bring the vision, mission, and values into everyday operations.

Your values come from YOU. So when everyone is on board and living the values, you can step away knowing that your clients are getting taken care of as YOU would take care of them.

For me, I know that members in The Opulence System™ are getting the same experience they would with any coach in my organization. Because we all live by the same values. My values, and the values we've created together as a team has been encapsulated into the business' DNA.

Now, at the beginning of your business journey, your values will come from you. That's logical - you're the only one there!

But as your business grows, and your team grows, it takes on a life of its own. Your values will evolve as your organization becomes more mature and complex.

You'll know how to get the right people on board after you read Chapter 11, but for now just let your values come from you. What do YOU want? How do YOU want to operate?

The true cost of culture rot

An employee who isn't aligned with the values of your business isn't going to last. Not only that, they have the capacity to start a rot from within. A values misalignment creates a toxic culture where poor results are the norm.

Whereas values alignment creates a *family*. Money is not the key driver for your staff to stick around. They're there because they enjoy it. They experience emotional rewards for being part of bringing the company's vision to life.

And I don't have to tell you, happy, engaged, and motivated staff are a hell of a lot more productive than those that are just there for the paycheck.

Think of mega-companies like Zappos, Google, and Twitter. They're all phenomenal companies with an amazing culture. It's not just about the perks - they offer their employees a range of other intangible benefits such as allowing them to be autonomous, they're made to feel a part of the big vision for the company, and that their contribution makes a difference.

Most of these mega-companies hiring strategies are based 50% on values match and culture fit, and 50% on skills and training. Zappos even pays new employees $2k to QUIT after their first week of training if they don't feel they're going to be a good fit for the business.

Now, $2k can seem a bit excessive. But Zappos know that the cost to onboard and train staff far outweighs that amount. As well as the additional cost of replacing them when they eventually leave. Not to mention the dip in productivity that occurs during the changeover time from offboarding an employee and onboarding a new one.

So in the long run, paying someone $2k not to waste their time and money is a bargain.

The yardstick for measuring performance

Your values don't just help you hire the right people. They also help you say *sayonara* to the wrong people.

Most firing conversations go like this:

"You're not performing well. I've decided to let you go." "What? I had no idea. This is ridiculous. How could you do this to me?"

The problem is that when most business owners have 'The Firing Conversation', it usually comes from a place of accusation. Even if they deliver the news as gently as possible, when you say someone isn't cutting the mustard, it's easy for them to get defensive. After all, they feel they've been attacked.

But when you shift that conversation around how that employee is living the values, it's a much easier exit. For both parties!

When Matt fired his toxic employee, the process was actually much simpler (and less painful) than he had built up in his head. "I simply kept bringing the conversation back to our values, and asking how he felt his performance rated against each of them," he told me later.

"When the guy rated himself poorly against one of our values and I asked him how he felt about that, he said 'I feel like I should find another job'."

Why was this conversation so much easier than Matt first imagined? It's because the values aren't personal - they're *behavioural*. They're a yardstick. Employees operate in tune with the values, or they don't. If they are let go, it's not because of some shortfall in their own personality, it's because there's not a good values-match.

Instead of a conversation that comes from a place of judgment ('you're not good enough to work here anymore'), it's a conversation around a *universal truth* ('you don't want to operate in the same way that we do'). That's a softer pillow to land on, isn't it?

We'll get more into hiring and firing in Chapter 11. But for now, just remember that your values make firing conversations more like an agreement to part ways, and less like a traumatic relationship breakup!

Business values vs personal values

Have you ever sat down and given thought to what your personal values are? Most people don't. We are so busy leading our lives that we don't stop and think 'do I really want this?'

That's where a lot of mid-life crises come from - people live their lives how they *think* they should live - according to their peers, society or whatever. And then they get to middle age and realise they're miserable.

If you're wondering what the difference is between your business values and your personal values... there isn't really any difference. You'll bring your personal values into your business and amplify them to fit the whole enterprise. These values shape the business culture and set the standard for how you will operate.

Besides, your business is part of YOU. You're not a 'clock in, clock out' employee working towards someone else's dream.

Your business is your baby. It's your blood sweat and tears. Your sacrifice. Your pride.

Why *wouldn't* you operate your business according to your own personal values? How do you expect to feel energized and fulfilled by what you do, if it doesn't align with what you value in life?

Building trust within yourself

Here's where the importance of defining your values really packs a punch.

If we don't trust our heart, and if we don't trust our intuition... then that means we're not trust*worthy*.

Think about it. If we're willing to sacrifice our standards and values, why the hell should we expect others to trust us?

If you're content with not living by values and standards in your business, you'll echo that same attitude in everything else in your life. You can't show up in the business environment a certain way, and another environment another way... you're *one* person. One heart. One set of values.

Therefore when it comes to us setting and achieving goals, how could you ever expect to follow through to completion if you're not first following through on your values and standards?

This realisation has been a massive Game Changer for me.

I find that if I'm showing up in alignment with my values, my standards, my beliefs... when I set a goal I have *absolute certainty* I'm going to achieve it.

If I say I'm going to achieve a goal, I 100% believe it. Because everything else I say in my life is true. I'm in alignment with my heart and mind.

There are no mental blocks or limiting beliefs in my way. I trust and believe in myself and my intention.

By living according to my values, I've conditioned my conscious and unconscious mind, that whatever I say, I DO.

By not sacrificing my standards, I've built trust with myself. I've strengthened my own self-belief.

You can too.

And I also have evidence that backs up this self-belief, because I've been operating in this way for some time. Which means that every goal I achieve adds to the evidence pile that this way of existing in the world WORKS.

Living according to my personal values WORKS for me. Who would've thought?

Where others lower their standards (or have no standards at all), and are buffeted by the absolute shitstorm that dictates their lives; once you align with your values, your path clears and you are unstoppable.

What values aren't

It's time to take action on what you've learned in this chapter. But before you get started on your values exercise, let's clear up one last thing.

I think that there's some fundamental values that we as human beings should all share. So when I see a business saying one of their values is honesty, that is a red flag to me. Because honesty should be a given. Integrity should be a given.

If you need a values poster on the wall reminding you to be honest and operate with integrity… you probably shouldn't be in business!

So when you're creating your values, be careful not to simply pay lip service to buzz words that sound cool, but are actually kind of empty. Think of the reason behind your choice of that value, and ask yourself if it really comes from your heart.

For example, at The Game Changers our values are

H - ave fun

E - veryone contributes

A - lways at cause

R - ealise our potential

T - ogether we grow

As well as being presented in a cool acronym that sneaks in another big value (do everything from the heart), these values guide everything we do at The Game Changers.

Have fun: Remembering to not get too serious and enjoy the ride!

Everyone contributes: All team members' ideas and opinions are heard and valued.

Always 'at cause': We take responsibility for what we create, both good and bad.

Realize our potential: Being our best selves, so we can help our members unlock theirs.

Together we grow: When the team is aligned, we are an unstoppable force. We take care of each other first, above everything else.

You can see that these values clearly outline how we want to do business. People who aren't our kind of client or partner are easy to identify.

The best part?

We attract other people who identify with our values. This makes doing business a whole lot easier and more enjoyable!

Setting your compass

Now you understand the essence of why values are so important. They're your internal compass, your yardstick, your standards, your DNA, your vibe...

They're the beating heart of your business.

It's time to set your *own* values.

Remember your vision and mission will change as you journey through the stages of building a business that works without you.

Your values will keep you aligned with who you are and what you want. They are also how you attract the right clients, A-player staff, and other business opportunities that fit perfectly with your vision and mission.

They're not just fancy words to put on a wall. They're active intentions for how the business is run, what it does, and how it does it.

Time to get into your dream zone again...

So what are the values you want your business to represent?

What type of culture do you want to create for your business family?

Where do you want to draw your 'lines in the sand'?

Take 20 minutes to go and think about this now. As always, there's a worksheet for you at www.pathtofreedom.com.au/resources

STEP 1: DREAM

This first section is a values elicitation exercise. When you ponder these questions, just be open to what comes up for you. And jot it down. Once again, there are no right or wrong answers.

1. What is the culture you wish to create within your business?

Is it fun? Energetic? Creative? Determined? Playful? What does it look like for you?

2. What are the standards you wish to set for yourself, your team, your business?

All good values start with YOU. What do you want to bring to your team and your company? What will you be proud of leaving behind as your legacy?

3. What are the behaviours you wish to exhibit and for your team members to exhibit?

Think about the non-negotiables - what is and isn't acceptable behaviour?

4. Can you follow through on the behaviours and standards you wish to create for yourself and the business?

There's no point creating values you can't follow through on a daily basis. Be honest, be realistic. There's no points for trying to be someone you're not. Plus the fastest way to create distrust within your team and clients is to say a value is important to you, but in reality your behaviour doesn't tell the same story.

STEP 2: CREATE

What are the 5 values you have decided on for your business?

Write them down. Put them somewhere you can see them often, and let them sit with you over the next few days.

After you've built the foundational pieces of your business - your vision, mission, and values, it's time to get started with the real juicy stuff. In the next chapter, we're going to put some solid steps in place for making your vision a reality.

THE PATH TO FREEDOM

YOUR GOALS

YOUR GOALS

"Where attention flows, energy goes and results show."

T. Harv Eker

Have you ever set a goal and not achieved it… and then felt like crap about it?

We humans love to set goals. We love to imagine having better lives and being better versions of ourselves. But we're often not so keen on actually doing what it takes to achieve our grand plans.

Goals are easy to set during the heady champagne fizz of New Years' eve, or after watching a TV infomercial promising *you too can get rock-hard abs by working out for just 5 minutes a day!*

But as soon as most goals are set, they start to fade. The reality of the work required to reach that goal sinks in. And we start hitting the snooze button. Gym shoes lie unused. Our *fantastic ab-tastic* exercise machine becomes a nesting spot for the cat. And we slip back into our old, comfortable habits.

Why do we fail to follow through on our goals so often?

Why do we give up on most New Year's resolutions just 3 weeks into the year?

Why do 85% of gym memberships get discarded?

It's not necessarily laziness or even an unwillingness to change. A lot of the time we give up on our goals simply because we made them without a real understanding of what it would take to achieve them.

I had a love-hate relationship with goal setting for the first 18 years of my time in business. And even longer than that personally. I had endless lists filled with goals. I'd dream up goals in the car. In meetings. On walks. In waiting rooms. My ambition was roaring with hunger… but I didn't know how to properly feed it.

Without a clear plan to achieve them, my goals were essentially just words on a list. Sadly, that's where many of them remained.

When I didn't achieve a goal, I'd just change the goal. "Oh, that was the wrong goal for me," I'd say to myself. "I want something else now." I kept moving the finish line, or changing the rules, or otherwise stuffing about.

The thing is, <u>without a map, every direction looks good.</u>

By flipping my attention from half-finished goal to half-finished goal, not only did I waste a lot of time, but I also ended up building a business that was utterly out of control. Because my goals were made on-the-fly, rather than being part of a system designed to help me reach my ultimate outcome (my vision).

If your goal achievement record is sporadic, it's time to do something different.

In this chapter, you're going to set *achievable* and *realistic* goals that will actively - and rapidly - move your business towards your ultimate vision. Then you're going to break those goals down and quantify the exact resources you'll need to achieve them (time, money, and people), and reverse-engineer a clear path to achieving them - step-by-step, in 45 minute blocks of time.

If that sounds like a lot of work, it's not. Systemizing your goals like this is actually quite simple. And it's incredibly effective.

This method of goal planning is the reason why at The Game Changers, we now hit our goals every single time. It's also the reason why The Opulence System™ members are able to complete projects that systemize their business to scale rapidly, tripling their revenue and doubling their time off within 12 months.

Once you understand the system, it's literally plug-n-play.

You see, goals are no different from an operating procedure or process document within your business.

When you think about it, we actually have processes around everything we do in life. When we get in the car, we have a pre-takeoff process (seat-belt, mirrors, ignition). We have a process around how to cook our favorite meal. A process around how to make the perfect cup of coffee...

- Boil water to 85 degrees.

- Take Garfield *'I hate Mondays'* mug from dish shelf.

- Put 1 sachet of sweetener into mug.

- Get teabag from kitchen cupboard 3rd shelf.

- Pour boiling water into mug until ¾ full… and so on.

- (Sorry to hardcore purist tea drinkers about the teabag).

Breaking down processes into individual steps creates a blueprint for someone else to do the same task, and get the same result.

In business, we have a process around how to open up the showroom in the morning, how to direct a call to the right person, how to send a calendar invite, and so on. Processes can be as simple or complex as they need to be, depending on what needs to be achieved.

The whole point of a process is that if we follow it step by step, then the outcome should always be the same. And if the outcome is not what's required, then we simply adjust the process until we get the results we want.

We'll dive deeper into processes in chapter 9.

For now, just know that goals are very much like processes. A lot of business owners set goals without taking the time to go and create the path to get there. But with no clear path or plan, how could you realistically expect to achieve the goal?

As the saying goes, 'if you fail to plan, you plan to fail'.

This chapter is where the foundational elements we laid in previous chapters start to become more tangible. As you apply this planning, you'll start transforming your goals from vague concepts into real-world actions that produce results you can see.

Why goals fail

Have you ever made a goal for the month or quarter, and then scrambled like crazy towards the end because you ran out of time?

Lack of planning leads to last minute rushes and ultimately, failure to achieve what you set out to do. It means setting 3, 6 or 12 month goals, while not actually doing anything to work towards them until toward the end when it's too late.

Sometimes we set goals that look too big to attempt. So we experience overwhelm because it seems like getting there is impossible.

Or we simply get caught in the whirlwind of business - those day to day activities that never stop. Ringing phones. Emails. Meetings. Clients. Putting out spot-fires. It's easy to get lost inside the machine.

If you're setting more goals than you're achieving, there could be a few other factors also at play…

Giving up too early

One of my earlier mentors was a billionaire who owned a bunch of car yards in Perth. I remember one day he said something profound to me:

"Barry, the goal should never be the variable. The variable should always be how much time, attention, and effort you're willing to put into achieving your goals."

I think many business owners have the same attitude to goals that I used to long ago… if I didn't achieve the goal, I'd just change the goal. What I really needed to do was reassess how I was organizing my resources around that goal to achieve it. But I was impatient.

The thing is, people typically overestimate what they can do over a short time, and underestimate what they can do over a long time.

So they give up. Often when they're 20 meters from the finish line.

Succeeding in business long-term is all about delayed gratification. The more you can embrace this fact, the better off you'll be.

Think about where you're sitting right now. Or standing. Maybe you're listening to this as an audiobook in your car. Wherever you are, pick a landmark near you. The TV. The nearest door. The backyard pool. Whatever.

If you take a step towards it right now, will you get there? No. At least, not instantly. But if you keep stepping towards that landmark, eventually you'll reach it.

For example at The Game Changers, in mid-2019 we set a goal to reach 100 members in The Opulence System™ by the end of that year.

Instead of taking 6 months to reach that goal, we actually took 9 months to get there. But the transformation the business went through in order to reach that goal means that we're now set to double that number in a much shorter time. Because we've now laid the right foundations to scale the business faster (kind of like you're doing as you work through this book).

If we'd thrown our Christmas party hats in the dirt and given up on our unachieved goal back in December, we wouldn't have *ever* reached our goal. And we'd probably still be feeling pretty down about it.

Instead, we didn't stop just because things weren't going perfectly to plan. We stayed the course, kept putting one foot in front of the other as we walked up the mountain.

Too many goals

Most business owners live with scattered focus. They are not sure what they need to be working on most, so get swept up in the whirlwind of business and don't get anywhere (except to Burnout City). Or they try to focus on many things at once, but move forward at a snail's pace because they never gain enough traction to actually see significant movement.

Imagine you've got 20 goals you're trying to achieve at once… what would your results look like? Do you think you'd move forward with ANY of them? Or would you have a dusty old folder of projects that have been sitting around your office for a year (or more)?

Trying to achieve too many goals at once is like trying to thread 20 Cheezels onto one hand - there's just not enough fingers to go around.

Just like we have limited Cheezel ring-fingers, we have limited time and attention too. Let's say for argument's sake that you've got 20 units of time each week. And you've got 20 goals. That means that you can only spend 1 unit of time on each goal per week.

But if you're chasing just one, two or three goals, you can invest more units of time into achieving each of those goals. Which means you'll achieve them far faster than trying to inch your way forward on 20 at once.

Perhaps the worst part about having many goals and seeing no progress is that it's incredibly deflating to never achieve what you set out to do! How utterly depressing. No wonder people give up.

Lengthy goal-cycles

A large part of your business success depends on your ability to move fast, be agile, and keep up with what the market is doing.

With business moving so quickly these days, it's important you don't tie yourself up in a big year-long goal. Instead, break one big goal into smaller, milestone projects. That way you can stay in touch with what's happening within your market, and pivot and adjust where necessary.

If your targets are set for 12+ months from now, it's easy for your organization to fall behind in the market. By that time it's too late to make the adjustments you need to. You have no idea what needs to be changed, dropped or improved... and you can essentially end up with no business at all.

I once knew a guy who had a great idea for a digital advertising business. He would create software that can display custom advertising on TV screens for medical offices, reception areas, hotel lobbies, restaurants... any business that could benefit from showing visitors special offers and promotions as they waited to be served.

He spent 18 months working with a software developer to complete his goal: a working prototype.

But when it was finally ready, the market had moved beyond him. Big companies had moved faster and taken the lion's share. What's more, display technology had advanced so when this guy's technology was finally finished... it was already out of date.

That's why The Opulence System™ works in 90-day cycles. 90 days works really well because the period is not too long, and not too short. The goals achieved over a quarter are big and meaningful enough to have a big impact within the business, but also they don't take too long to achieve. So you can recalibrate as needed along the way to account for a changing market.

That's not to say you shouldn't plan 1 year, 5 years, and 10 years ahead. You should. And you will in this chapter. But by setting 90-day milestone projects, it's easier to move forward faster, and pivot when necessary.

Unrealistic goals

As I reflect on my own journey over the past 18 years in business, I realize that I was way too ambitious when I first got into the game. When I started my first business, I had all of these goals of turning over millions of dollars, buying a bunch of properties, and building my business to a certain position... but the reality was that I had no prior experience in business.... and no idea what it would take to actually get there.

I was basing my goals on an illusion... I saw other successful business owners and aspired to be like them, but I had no tangible understanding of what was required from both an effort perspective, from a resources perspective, and most importantly from an emotional and psychological perspective.

I thought that if I just worked hard, I could simply *force* the goal to happen. But my goals didn't reflect the reality of how I was positioned at the time.

There's no point setting a goal of closing 100 clients in 3 months if you've only closed 10 in the last month. Lots of business owners think that more volume is the answer to every problem. They think if they want to 10x their results, they just 10x their ad spend, 10x their number of sales calls, or something like that.

It doesn't work that way.

In my early 20s, I had a friend who worked part-time in his Uni's science lab. One Saturday he was there organizing and processing samples. He was in a hurry to get out and enjoy his afternoon, but had a last batch to put through a centrifuge.

"Surely if I spin the centrifuge at twice the speed, it will be done in half the time, right?", he figured.

As you might imagine, spinning the samples at twice the speed required didn't lead to faster results, it just led to a bunch of ruined samples. (And a lot of explaining to do.)

In business, it's kind of the same. Progress is not as simple as 1+1=2. Business works on a compounding scale, not a linear one.

For example, every time you hire another staff member into your business, the complexity of the organization increases by *three*, not by one. This is due to the extra intricacy in your business' communication stream. I'll unpack this more in Chapter 11.

But there's one key element of team management that directly impacts your chances of achieving a goal…

People confusion and misalignment

When your team doesn't know what they're all working towards, you just have a bunch of people working at odds with each other.

Do you remember the case study you read at the end of Chapter 3? To jog your memory, Jackson was working with 2 co-directors. Before aligning everyone in the company vision, mission and values, the directors of his business were all working towards their own goals, based on their own personal priorities. Which created friction, lack of cohesion and poor results.

When your goals are small, manageable, bite-sized tasks with measurable targets and deadlines, it's easy to communicate them to your employees. They know what's required over the next 90 days. Then everyone starts to align themselves around the business' highest priorities, and propel you forward faster and easier.

Your 90 day goals are like little sprints that generate tangible results quickly. This is not only a great motivator for you, but for your team as well.

Giving up too often

Years ago I had a realization: if I never followed through on my word, not only was I essentially lying to others, but I was also conditioning my own mind to believe that I'm full of B.S.

On the flip side, I realized that if I follow through on the things I tell people I'm going to do, I'm conditioning myself - both consciously and unconsciously - that I'm a man of my word.

Consistency is the way to build trust. And it works both ways...

If you're saying to your partner you're going to be home at 6pm, and you constantly stay at the office until 7 or 8... you're letting *both* of you down.

If you're saying to your team that you're going to implement a new initiative that will make their jobs easier, more fun, or whatever, and you don't follow through.... you're letting your team down.

The worst part? The more you fail to follow through on the promises you make, the more the people around you lose trust in you.

The fastest way to make your team start to lose faith in your leadership ability is to regularly break your own word. To fail to do things you say you're going to do. Others pick up on that lack of integrity and lower their expectations of you, their role, and the business. And that's when culture rot starts to seep in. Because they feel they're working for a flake.

What do you think that's doing to our self worth? Our self-confidence? Our self-belief? It's breaking it apart, piece by piece. Whether we realize it or not. And the more it's shattered, the harder it is to regain. It's a vicious cycle.

But as I said before, it goes both ways.

Regularly following through on completing goals builds a feedback loop of success. The more cycles you feed into that loop, the stronger it gets.

Every time I follow through on a goal, I build up my *commitment to completion* muscle. These days whatever goal I set for myself, my internal system knows nothing else but to follow through.

There is no other option. No flaking out. No giving up. No letting myself get distracted by some shiny object. And that's incredibly powerful.

Understanding your goal hierarchy

Remember before when I said achieving goals is like following any other process (such as making a cup of tea)? You're about to learn the structure that we at The Game Changers have used to help 100s of our clients create rapid momentum for building businesses that work without them.

Everything is systemized, so each goal, project, and task feeds into the bigger 10-year goals that, in turn, bring the business closer to its vision.

Looking at the diagram below, you can see 1-year wildly important goals (WIGS), 10-year big hairy audacious goals (BHAGS), and 4 x 90-day goals. 90-day goals are broken up into projects, which are broken down into tasks.

Everything feeds the bigger outcome above it:

- Your tasks help complete your projects.

- Your projects help complete your 90-day goals.

- Your 90-day goals help complete your 1-year WIGs.

- Your WIGs help to complete your 10-year BHAGs.

- Your BHAGs help to bring you closer to your ultimate vision.

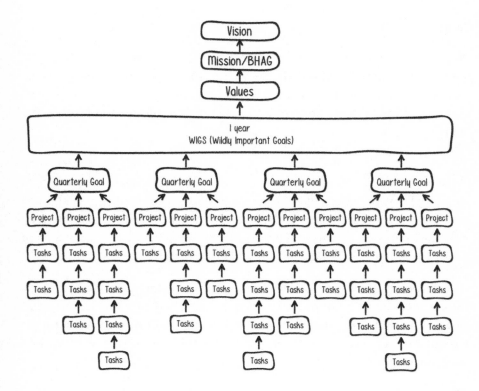

This is where you start to see the importance of the framework behind the vision, mission, and values - they determine your goals. Your goals then determine your projects and daily tasks.

Setting these may look like a lot of work. But as I said earlier, it's not. And it's actually quite fun.

In The Opulence System™, we sit down with members for 2 days every quarter to plan this out at our live Business Intensive events.

We review our 10-year goals - are they still aligned with our vision, mission, and values?

We revise our 1-year goals - these usually need tweaking because business grows and changes fast!

Then we spend half a day breaking down our 1-year goals into 90 day projects, and those projects are then broken down into milestones, tasks, and responsibilities.

Within this 90 day planning, we reflect on the last quarter - the good, the bad and the ugly. What did we do well? What didn't we do well? What needs to happen to fix whatever's not working? We take this all into account when setting up our next 90 days' projects and operational activities.

At the end of the Business Intensive event, The Opulence System™ members have a clear blueprint of where they're headed over the next quarter. They know exactly what needs to be done on a daily, weekly, and monthly basis to reach their goals. They know which staff members will be responsible for each project and the tasks within it. They also have a good idea of how much ROI each project will bring to their business.

The best part: they know that their projects are bringing them closer to their 1-year goals. And their 1-year goals keep them on track for their 10-year goals. Their 10-year goals keep them on track for fulfilling their ultimate vision. All they have to do is hit their daily tasks and the rest will fall into place in a Domino-like effect.

Done this way, goal setting is a powerful system that fuels rapid business innovation and improvement.

If you're a smaller business with less than 5 staff, you don't need to spend 2 days doing this. At The Game Changers we choose to, because it gets the best results for our The Opulence System™ members.

Goal setting can take 2 hours if you run a smaller operation. Get the team together for an afternoon and map your goals out together. Order some catering and make it a fun event. It *should* be fun - you're planning your future successes!

If your organization has considerably more staff and priorities, you can build this model out and include 10-year goals, 5-year goals, 3-year goals, and 1-year goals… whatever works for your level of business complexity. The point is that every goal is part of a chain of ascension towards your ultimate vision.

What makes a good goal?

A good goal should have a start point and an end point. Good goals are also specific and measurable.

For example:

We're going to increase our clients from 100 to 200 by April 2020
Or
We're going to increase our retention rate from 75% to 85% by July 2020
The above goals follow the criteria for success:

They're time-based
They're specific
They're measurable

Most importantly…they're realistic.
As I mentioned earlier, there's no point setting a goal of closing 100 clients in 3 months if you've only closed 10 in the last month. Look at the patterns behind you, and aim further ahead, but not ridiculously far. Think of your goals as *steps to success.*

When setting your projects:

- Make sure they are clearly defined, measurable and have a deadline

- Give them a good, better, best target

- Set no more than 2-3 each quarter (depending on the size of your team - I'll cover this a bit later in this chapter)

Setting your first goals

The goal here (pun intended) is to systemize your goal setting, so your goals don't stay dreams on a notepad, but become actionable plans that are easy to follow.

STEP 1: GOAL DUMP

The goal dump is basically a brainstorm session. It's about getting your ideas out of your head, and onto paper. You can do this either by yourself, or get your team involved.

Grab a piece of paper and write every idea you have about improving your business. A good framework to follow is to think within the fundamental areas of business.

These fundamental areas are:

Marketing

Sales

Fulfillment

People performance

Financials

So start there. Divide your paper into 5 columns if that works for you. Use a piece of paper for each department if that's your style. Or download the handy worksheet we've created for you at www.pathtofreedom.com.au/resources.

You can use a whiteboard if you are working with your team. But if you're doing this solo, use a piece of paper instead of a digital device. There's something about writing on paper that opens the brain up more than typing onto a screen can. Studies have found that writing out ideas manually slows us down, forces us to pay closer attention to the words we write, and triggers creativity. So give it a try.

Don't self-edit. Just write it all down. There are no dumb ideas here. Nothing is impossible. Just get every idea in your head out. Everything you want to do, think you should do, or feel you have to do…. just get it down.

STEP 2: CHOOSE A THEME

After doing your goal dump, look for the patterns and themes within your ideas.

What areas are you focusing on most? (eg: marketing, sales, fulfillment, etc)

What common themes have you identified?

Do your ideas relate back to your 10-year BHAGs (your mission)?

Which ideas will have the most positive impact on your BHAGs?

By identifying priorities and themes, you can start seeing the bird's eye view of what your business needs to move forward. This allows you to focus all your energies on the right things, in the right order, and finally see business growth and evolution towards your ultimate vision.

At The Game Changers, our goals are always around these key themes:

1. Client acquisition (our lead generation and conversion processes)

2. Client retention (client happiness and results)

3. Team and culture (aligning our people and business results)

This helps us stay focused on where we're going in terms of growing our community, in terms of serving our community, and in terms of business operations. If we always keep our goals focused on these three areas, we know that our business will stay on the right track.

Now, each business is different. While The Game Changers has the three focus areas I mentioned above, your business might need to focus on other areas. For us, these three themes work.

Your theme might be on making more sales, or improving your service delivery. It might be to free up better cash flow to use in R&D projects. It might be a people overhaul, or building a new culture within your business. The more goals you dump onto your page, the easier it will become to notice themes that guide you.

STEP 3: DEFINE YOUR 1-YEAR WIGS AND 90-DAY GOALS

The core question you need to ask here is: "If everything was to stay the same, and I could change ONE thing this year to move my business towards my 10-year goal, what would that one thing be?"

Narrow your list until you have defined one to three wildly important goals (WIGS). If you are a solo operator, you should probably focus on just one. If you are a bigger organization, you probably have the resources (time, money, people) to spend on more WIGS.

When you have your shortlist, it's time to split those WIGS into 90-day goals.

What things need to happen, and in what logical order, for the WIG's success criteria to be met?

Don't load up on too many 90-day goals. Stick with just one or two goals if you have less than 5 employees, or up to five goals if you're running a team of 10+ staff.

Not overloading your team with too many goals at once means you can implement faster. Which then means that you can see earlier if a particular project isn't having any effect on your goal.

How can you tell if a project isn't making an impact? Because you'll have feedback loops and KPIs for that particular goal. We'll cover KPIs more in chapter 8, but for now just lock it in your mind that each project has KPIs that indicate its level of success.

When you're finished, you will have defined your:

10-year goals (BHAGS)

1-year goals (WIGS)

90 day goals (let's call them SPRINTS)

Your goal structure should work on an ascension model. Like Russian dolls, each task feeds into a goal, which feeds into a bigger goal, and so on.

Look at your page for a minute.

Do your SPRINTS work toward your WIGS?

Do your WIGS help you achieve your BHAG?

Does your BHAG help you achieve your mission?
Does your mission still lead to your vision?

Remember your vision is your ultimate goal. Everything you do in your business must feed into that goal on some level. Otherwise, what are you doing all this for?

STEP 4: BREAK DOWN YOUR 90-DAY GOALS INTO PROJECTS

If you look at your 90-day goals for too long, it's likely you'll need an aspirin and a lie-down. They're big. They'll need a lot of work. It can get overwhelming.

Which is why we break up your 90-day goals into projects.

These projects then get broken down into clear, actionable tasks that only take 45 minutes each. We'll get into this a bit later in the chapter, but for now, we need to decide on what your quarterly projects will be.

Let's say one of our 1 year goals at The Game Changers is to increase our Opulence members to 200 members in 12 months. To achieve this, we'll need to enrol 66 members each quarter. So that becomes one of our 90-day goals.

But how will we achieve this 90-day goal? Well, we might decide on two projects that feed into that goal: one focused on a marketing campaign, and one on improving our sales conversions.

The entire goal-setting process simply involves reverse-engineering bigger tasks until you end up with the smallest unit of time and effort possible.

One project = one person

If your business is smaller than a team of five, then you should have a maximum of three projects to ONE goal… ideally less. Because you need to have a single point of accountability for each project. And you don't want to overload your team.

If you assign more than one person, accountability gets diluted. People assume the other person will 'take care of it'. At the end of the day, you've just got a group of people pointing fingers at each other.

So keep a single point of accountability for each project. Sure, you can have more than one person working on each project. But one person is accountable for making sure the end result is achieved.

For us at The Game Changers, we have three goals each quarter, and three projects within each goal. So we're running 9 projects at any one time across three goals, which are aligned with our focus (client acquisition, client retention, team + culture). Our team can handle this among the other responsibilities and activities within their role.

Here's what it might look like for your business:

1-year WIG:	Quarterly Goal:	Project 1: Build and launch new Facebook ads funnel
200 Members in Opulence by April 2021	Generate 500 New sales leads	Project 2: Implement a referral program
		Project 3: Create a Joint Venture with another industry leader

Remember this is a process - you may not have the 'perfect' project in mind right now. That's ok. Just go with what looks best right now.

As time goes by, your priorities will change anyway. Business is always changing. The most important thing is that you move forward. Fail to act, and you'll stagnate and your business will die.

Lead vs Lag projects

Many years ago in my kitchen and bathroom installation business, I gave my sales team an individual target of hitting $1 million each per year. After I gave them this target, I noticed their performance started wilting.

How was this so? I was looking after them, I was incentivizing them, I was giving them plenty of leads to convert... what was going on?

I soon realized that I'd scared the hell out of them by giving them such a massive target. They made good money each week, but the number 'one million' was a seemingly unachievable task for them. So they sabotaged their progress because they simply couldn't imagine hitting this frighteningly massive goal.

Eventually I realized my problem was giving them a *lag measure* goal.

A *lag measure* is a result you were trying to achieve in the past. By the time you get the data, the result has already happened. You can't change it or influence it. By the time you address it, it's done and dusted.

Whereas a *lead measure* is an activity that drives the result that leads to the lag measure. Lead measures are predictable and controllable.

For example, the weight you see when you jump on a scale is a *lag* measure. It's there, and there's nothing you can do to change that number - at least, not right then and there. Whereas exercising 5 hours a week, and limiting your calories to 1500 a day - those are *lead* measures. They are things that you can change to influence that number on the scales in the future.

Thinking about this problem with my team, I asked myself: 'what are the lead measures I can influence to get the result I want?' (Which was $1 million in sales per year - the lag measure).

So I broke down the goal into milestones, steps, and tasks.

We sold kitchens costing approximately $22k. That meant to meet their $1 million dollar goal, my team needed to make $88k per month. That's a milestone of 4 kitchens a month.

Ok, that's a bit more manageable... but still kind of overwhelming.

So I broke the numbers down even further. I looked at my KPIs and found that I had a 50% quote-to-close rate. So to make 4 sales a month, my team had to send out 8 quotes a month. Getting easier...

When I reframed my team's goal from 'make a million bucks a year' to 'send out 2 quotes a week', that new goal seemed so easily achievable the team went out and smashed it.

Soon they were hitting that million-dollar goal easily - thanks to simply focusing a lead measure and breaking it down into small tasks.

How to choose the right projects for your goal

There's no absolute way to know if your project is actually going to work or not. If it was that easy to back a winner, we'd all be rolling in riches. Some projects will flourish, some will flounder.

Over the years I've put my efforts into many projects that didn't work out. That's just the nature of business. You've got to try different things to find out what works (and doesn't work).

That being said, there is a tool I use with my team to assess where we should be spending our resources each quarter. That tool is called The Opportunity Evaluator™.

It's a spreadsheet where you write down all the ideas you've got, and then estimate:

1. What sort of time investment it would take to complete

2. What capital investment would be needed to complete the project (eg: spending money on marketing, contracts etc)

3. What is the potential yield - how much could you make?

Then you calculate the potential ROI for each idea:

hours x hourly rate + expenses / potential yield

That gives you a percentage of what to expect. Obviously these figures aren't set in stone because they're all estimates - but they do serve as a good early indication of which ideas carry the most weight.

You can download your copy of The Opportunity Evaluator™ at this link: www.pathtofreedom.com.au/resources

If you haven't got a lot of time right now, but you've got some money, you might want to launch a project that doesn't require much time, but offers a good yield if you invest some cash. Such as paid advertising.

What if you haven't got much money, but you've got time? Then you want to invest in a project that doesn't cost much but takes some time to get off the ground. Search engine optimization (SEO) fits into this category.

If you have no money and no time, there are still options. The decision then comes down to weighing up your priorities and resources, and finding a happy medium. It's not an exact science, but it's still a hell of a lot better than pure guesswork.

Remember to focus on lead measures - things that can be influenced. Your 1-year and 90-day goals are lag measures. When you look at your results, it will be too late to do anything about it. Lead measures help you get in front of the goal and influence it before its deadline.

When you launch each completed project, you go back to the Opportunity Evaluator™ and add your results. How much time and money did they take? What was your ROI?

The more you start recording these numbers, the better you will become at estimating which projects you should focus on at any given time. Over time, you'll train your brain to think more strategically and realistically around project inputs and yields.

For me, I used the Opportunity Evaluator™ a lot 4 or 5 years ago. Now I don't need to - I've developed the skill of evaluating projects myself and pretty much instinctively know where to focus first.

As with most things in life, the more you do it, the better at it you get.

STEP 5: DEFINE YOUR TASKS - YOUR 'STEPS TO COMPLETION'

By this point, your mind is probably swirling with goals and projects. Don't get overwhelmed, because I'm about to share with you a simple way of breaking them down into easily manageable, bite-sized pieces.

First, write every step to completion down on a Post-It note. Use different colors to visually categorize your steps if you're that kind of person.

The task on each sticky note should take no longer than 45 minutes to complete. Schedule working stretches longer than that, and you'll get brain fade.

Research shows that the optimal working time is 45 minutes of focused work, then with a 15-minute break. Francesco Cirillo's Pomodoro technique is the most famous - the technique uses a timer to break work into intervals 25 minutes long, separated by short breaks.

I find that this formula works best for me:

- 45 minutes focused work with no distractions
- Then a 10 minute break
- 5 minutes to prepare for what is coming next

When you've written every task down, put all your notes on a wall, window, or whiteboard - this is your scrum board.

Arrange them in order, and then put your sticky note tasks into the 'to do' column, and move the ones you're working on now into the 'doing' column.

Here's what it might look like for setting up a Facebook ads campaign:

	TO-DO	DOING	DONE
Test landing page	Research competitor ads	Gathering images for ads	Setup Facebook ads account
Write emails sequence	Write ad copy	Install Facebook pixel	
Create ad images	Setup retargeting	Define audiences	
Final proof LP			

Every week, as you complete tasks, move each sticky note to the 'done' section of your scrum board. Then move others up the line. And so on.

Keeping the 'done' sticky notes is a really powerful motivator.

Visually seeing those sticky notes gradually building up in your 'done' column combats any urges you're feeling to go and find a shiny object that's going to give you instant gratification. It shows you that you ARE making progress, and gives you a boost of commitment to completion.

This method also allows you to manage your resources: time, money and people.

Just say there are 13 sticky note steps for your project. Each sticky note represents one hour of your time. You know that to complete this project, you'll need to dedicate one hour a week, for 13 weeks in the quarter.

When you're managing a project on your own, it's easy to schedule those hours into your calendar. Mark them off and guard them with the same determination as you would a client meeting.

Because the time you're spending on these projects is actually the most important time you have within your business. It's high-level projects and planning that will allow you to scale your business and live the lifestyle you want - not the day-to-day level stuff.

Using a scrum board with your team

The sticky note scrum board works great for me because I'm a very visual person. So for projects that only I am working on, it works perfectly.

When you're managing a team, the sticky note scrum board needs to get a little more sophisticated.

If everyone works in the same office, you might choose the 'big whiteboard' option. For bigger projects and teams, you absolutely need to use software to manage all the moving parts.

At The Game Changers, and for many other businesses with remote staff, online tools are your best friend for organizing your team around their projects and goals.

We use Asana to get everyone on the same page around a project and assign individual tasks to team members. There are many other options out there - just do a quick Google search for 'project management tool' and find which work best for you.

Whatever software you choose, once you set up your project as 'virtual sticky notes', you'll understand how many hours you need to find, and in which teams. For example, just say I look at my projects and I see 36 sticky notes. That means I need to budget for 36 hours, or 3 hours a week for the next 3 months, to get this project done.

If your project has a financial outlay, include that on your sticky notes too, so you know how much cash you need to earmark over the next 3 months.

If your project affects any team within your business, include it as well, so that the department can budget for any resources they need to provide.

Breaking down your projects like this isn't always an exact science. Things don't always go to plan. But it does give you a pretty accurate path to follow that will get you to your goal, sooner or later.

Building feedback loops

There's a character in the X-Men movies who is super-fast. So fast that when he runs around at hyper-speed, people around him barely move an inch.

This comes in pretty handy in a crisis, where there's guns firing and explosions and all the 'big boom' stuff going on. This guy just zips in, and moves people an inch to the left, an inch to the right, taking them out of the firing line (or in the case of bad guys, into the firing line), and so on.

A feedback loop kind of gives you this superpower when it comes to your goals. Instead of just firing the arrow and hoping it hits the target, a feedback loop lets you slow down time for a minute, so you can tap the arrow a bit to the left, or right… whatever gives it a better chance of hitting the bullseye.

Many business owners set out to achieve a certain goal, don't get there, and get pissed off and disheartened. Then they decide to change course, set another goal, or pursue another shiny object.

They fail to reflect and create a feedback loop in that reflection: looking back at where they started, where they were going, and where they are now. Then analyzing what has taken them closer to their goal, and what hasn't.

Feedback loops don't just exist in goal planning. Everything in your business should have a feedback loop, so it goes through a constant cycle of implementation, review, and readjustment. Leave anything alone in your business for too long, and it will go stagnant.

Every week you should be asking the question: Is the way I'm investing my time moving me closer to my goals, or pushing me further away?
And not just time. Your money, your emotions, your resources… what are you spending them on? Are those non-tangible purchases giving you the return you desire?

Thanks to feedback loops, you're always going to hit your goal. You may not hit it as soon as you first thought, or as easily as you imagined, but constantly recalibrating your approach to your goal means that some day, you will absolutely get there.

No more throwing everything you've got blindly at the wall and hoping something sticks. Let the feedback along the way guide your path, bit by bit.

Because in every feedback loop review, all you need to ask is:

What moved us closer to the goal?

What moved us further away?

Then you do more of what worked, and less of what didn't. It's as simple as that. We just tend to make goals way too complicated.

How to create feedback loops that keep your goals on track

Your feedback loop is part brainpower, part cold-hard-numbers.

As you plan out the tasks within each project, include a review period at regular intervals. They can be monthly, weekly... whatever works best for the project.

These reviews are for your team (or just yourself if you're operating solo) to get together and discuss the project's trajectory so far.

What's working?

What's more difficult than first imagined?

What problems are hindering the process?

What opportunities for a better result can we see?

And most importantly, is this project still going to help us reach our bigger goal?

Beyond the discussion, you have numbers. Numbers don't lie. You can build KPIs into every project that indicate whether the project is showing results, or needs to be reconsidered.

In The Opulence System™, we use a green light, amber light, red light system where each KPI has an acceptable range, an OK range, and a danger range.

For example, if you are building a new referral process and expect that you will be 80% finished in 2 weeks, yet in fact you're only 60% of the way after 2 weeks... that's an amber light.

If you're 20% finished in 2 weeks, that's a red light. Time to review what you're doing, and adjust your project parameters, resources, or something else. Straighten that arrow.

Quarterly Goal	Project	1 Month Milestone	1 Month Actual	Tasks
100 clients by April 21	New Facebook Ad Funnel	Setup complete 100%	Setup complete 80%	Yellow - review
Retention rate at 85% by May 2021	New onboarding process	Drafted and waiting setup 100%	Drafted 50%	Red - urgent review
Retention rate at 85% by May 2021	New training portal	wireframe built 100%	Complete 100%	Green - review at next milestone

Is unconscious patterning holding you back?

I had a client many years ago - let's call him Joe.

Joe had been in business for 10 years, and was doing ok. But his dream was to build a million-dollar recruitment business. When he signed up with me, his BHAG was to generate $100k in revenue a month.

At this point, Joe was turning over $35k per month. Three months after we started working together, he was at about $80k per month. But then something strange happened.

For two months after Joe started hitting $80k, nothing changed. All this incredible growth stopped dead in its tracks.

It baffled me. We'd gone through the steps of building a business that works without you. (Yes, the very same ones you're reading right now.) We'd implemented changes. We'd reorganized.

I just couldn't see any reason why Joe was smacking against his glass ceiling.

Then one day I had an idea. Could Joe be sabotaging his *own* success?

Joe was a super high-achiever. He'd had that $100k goal for years. In fact, it had been the main focus of his life for over a decade.

So I wondered if because there was no goal after the $100k... Joe was actually subconsciously stopping himself from reaching it? Joe had been focusing on that magic number for so long that he had no idea what he'd do after he got there.

In the words of Plutarch, (misquoted by the fabulously wicked Hans Gruber in Die Hard), 'When Alexander saw the breadth of his domain, he wept for there were no more worlds to conquer.'

So I decided to test my theory. I rang him up and said 'Joe, I've been thinking about your goal. And I think it's a bit small - let's aim for $150k a month.'

'Barry, but we haven't even hit $100k yet...'

'I know mate, but if we go for $150k, we're going to hit the $100k anyway, so why not aim a bit further?'

Joe decided to give my idea a go. We set our sights on $150k.

The next month, Joe got to $109k. BOOM. Absolutely flew straight past it. Just with one mindset shift.

Where focus goes, energy flows and results show.

Turning projects into operational activities

Let's just say one of our goals is to build a new Facebook ad funnel and send traffic through it.

Once that's executed and is working well, it becomes an Operational Activity. Optimizing the funnel, running traffic to the funnel… it's not a new project anymore, but is instead part of the daily activities within your business. It needs to be absorbed into your regular operational activities.

Before the Facebook ad funnel is created, it's a project. It's a growth activity to achieve a goal. After the funnel is built and working, you don't just shut it down. You maintain it. Like watering a garden.

Taking on the right operational activities is how you scale your business.

A lot of business owners spread their resources too thin over too many areas. Let's keep using the Facebook ads example. Instead of seeing one goal to completion (the creation of an ad funnel that gives consistent and excellent ROI), they'll focus on multiple social channels without actually measuring whether those activities are taking them closer to the results they want.

Now you know how to set goals that you'll actually achieve.

Does it seem like a lot of work to you?

Sure, it takes a little time. But this method of goal setting is actually less work than what you're most likely doing now. And it will give you the clarity and structure you need to get important stuff done. No more spending your days running around like a headless chicken.

We humans put a crapload of energy into procrastinating, worrying about what needs to be done, doing a whole bunch of other stuff that doesn't need to be done.

Most people are willing to work 40 hours to avoid a 2 hour task.

The more you do this goal planning, the more you will create an internal (mindset) and external (team) environment where you hit your goals, every month.

It's a fantastic feeling.

YOUR ORGANIZATIONAL CHART

YOUR ORGANIZATIONAL CHART

"Running a business doesn't mean running every department yourself. If the CEO has their finger in all the pies, that's a lot of critical points of failure. Remove them from the business, and nobody would know what to do. Which means the business is not actually viable."

Georgie Brooke - Greater Data

"*How* many people report to you?"

Game Changers coach Keith couldn't believe it. Surely he must have misheard?

"Fourteen," Georgie repeated. "I know that's probably too many."

Keith looked at Georgie like he was crazy.

"How do you get anything done? No wonder you don't sleep at night!"

The year was 2019, and Keith and Georgie were at our Business Intensive event at the Gold Coast. The room was humming with members of The Opulence System™ chatting during a short break from the day's learning.

"You should have no more than three to five people reporting to you right now," Keith said. "Eventually you'll need only one direct report."

Keith took out a pencil and sketched a new Organizational Chart on Georgie's notepad. But instead of all paths leading back to Georgie's door directly, he used a similar pyramid structure... but only one path led up to the top.

"When you organize your people and departments this way, your department heads are accountable for everything and everyone that falls under their umbrella." Keith advised. "Instead of you being responsible for 14 people, your department heads are responsible for a few people each."

"But who is responsible for the department heads? How will I know if they're doing what needs to be done?" Georgie asked. He was trying to take on board Keith's suggestion, but his inner control freak was throwing a fit.

"Your department heads are accountable for their people and results. Your *integrator* is accountable for the department heads. Essentially they manage your managers, and filter only the important information up to you. So you can spend your time and energy on high-level activities that improve the business, while still keeping your finger on the pulse. See?"

This was a Eureka moment for Georgie. Why hadn't he realized this before?

Georgie's team structure was a bit all over the place. He had a couple of managers already working in the business, but he was still coming to work wearing several hats every day. Because despite having *some* organizational structure in place, the accountabilities within that structure were all messed up.

Every day, Georgie bounced from product marketing, into sales, then finance, a bit of HR… he had a hand in every area. Although he had plenty of people working under him to get stuff done, Georgie was the one accountable for results company-wide. It all rested on him.

"I can't believe I didn't see this before," he said to Keith. "Right now, whenever there is a problem in the business, the accountability falls on me to resolve it. So I spend most of my life just fixing problems, not on the work that actually needs to be done."

Keith nodded and smiled.

"It also means that you're not getting the best out of your team," added Keith. "They rely on you for all the decision making and planning. What about their ideas? Surely your business would improve if you add some different perspectives into the mix?"

"You're right," Georgie agreed. "It's time to make some changes."

When the Business Intensive was over, everyone flew home buzzing with ideas and plans for improving their business. Georgie knew the first thing he needed to do.

When he got back to the office, he gathered his team together.

"How would you all feel if we reorganized things a bit?"

Georgie showed the team the new Organizational Chart he'd been working on during the plane ride home from the Gold Cost.

The looks on their faces said it all. *He finally gets it.*

In my first business building and installing kitchens, we always started with the blueprints. What was the layout of the house? Where did the kitchen fit in? What facilities needed to be installed (plumbing, gas), and where did they need to go?

If we had started by building a kitchen island in the middle of the room, and then built the rest of the kitchen around it, we'd have hit the wall (literally) at one point or another.

There would be no room for an oven. The sink would be in the wrong place. The window would be blocked by a pantry.

The result? A barely-functional kitchen.

Business owners often approach their business this way. They start with one role (their own), and build the business around that, hiring at random to fill needs as they arise. Frankensteining a business structure together this way is part of the reason why they end up with a business that isn't functioning optimally.

It's also the reason why, despite how many people they hire, these business owners still end up doing the lion's share of the work.

How many roles do you think you're covering in *your* business right now?

Think back through the last couple of weeks, and roughly categorize the types of things you were involved in.

Did you do any staff training?

Did you work on a new advertising campaign?

Did you handle any customer service issues?

Did you sort out a procurement problem?

Did you onboard any new clients?

If you are doing anything except thinking up cool ideas and managing high-level key relationships… you're doing too much.

How do you think entrepreneurs like Richard Branson manage multiple businesses at once? He's certainly not spending his time on the tarmac servicing his airplanes, or answering the phones at Virgin Galactic.

The reason Richard Branson and so many other entrepreneurs can run multiple mega-businesses comes down to this: <u>Having the right people in the right roles.</u>

Because the thing is, no matter what your vision is… you're going to need some help to achieve it.

So this chapter is about creating the framework of people you'll need to help you achieve your mission and vision.

You're going to map out all the roles your business will need to work towards these autonomously - that is, without you needing to be there to drive the ponies.

Similarly to how you mapped your goals, then reverse-engineered every step to get there, you're going to reverse-engineer a company structure that stands on its own.

While other businesses evolve organically, building walls and windows here and there as the need arrives, you're going to map out the rooms of your 'house'.

How big do they need to be? What will their exact purpose be? What other rooms do they need to be close to? How do they fit in with the layout of the whole structure?

In Three Little Pig terms, you're the one building the brick house.

As the fable goes, the brick house doesn't blow over easily. It's sturdy. It's not missing a wall or a supporting beam. Similarly, when your business is structured with the right roles and departments, there's no single point of failure.

That means if you or anyone else in your business disappear suddenly, the whole thing won't come crashing down. That's not to say it wouldn't be a big inconvenience if your marketing manager decides to run off to the circus. Sure, it would be a bit of a pain.

But the point is, you'll have the right systems and structures built around the role so that you can re-fill the position quickly and as hassle-free as possible.

Now, you might be thinking, 'But I'm only an organisation of one - what does this have to do with me? Surely my focus right now should be on generating leads and making sales!'

I absolutely believe that when you're turning over less than $500k per year, 80% of your time should be on sales and marketing. (If you're wondering what to do with the other 20%, focus on strategy, delivery, and financial management.)

But this book is all about putting in the frameworks so that when you grow, not only do you grow faster, but you scale easily too. So if you're a solo operator, this chapter will show you how to get it right from the beginning and grow faster.

Setting up your people power

Your Organisational Chart is essentially a map of the roles within your business.

Kind of like the family tree project you may have done back at school, your chart branches out from the top (Visionary - that's you) down through your Integrator, department heads, managers, and other task-based roles.

Most businesses will have the following departments:

>> Marketing

>> Sales

>> Fulfillment

>> People

>> Finances

Everything in your business falls into these categories. Your business might have a slightly different department layout than this. For instance, if you sell physical goods, your fulfillment department might be split into delivery and procurement.

But the essentials remain the same.

Not only do these departments inform your Organizational Chart, but they relate to how we set up our internal filing structure (we'll talk about this later this chapter), and our project management software (such as Asana - we'll talk about this more in chapter 10)

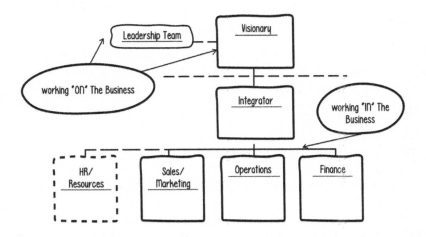

If you're a solo operator, or if your business is still in the startup phase, it's likely that your name will be in all of those boxes.

That's totally ok. When your business is turning over less than around $1.2 million a year, your focus is more around hustle. It's about getting things up and running so you can depend on your business to run profitably.

But know this: <u>your purpose as an entrepreneur is to remove yourself from every role except for visionary.</u> So your business can run independently of any one person's labour - including yours.

As you grow, you'll hire staff to fill each role in your Organizational Chart.

Later in this book, I'll give you a tool that helps you identify exactly what roles to hire for, and in what order.

For now, ask yourself this -

'For my business to reach its BHAGs, what departments and roles will I need?'

You've identified your BHAGs already in chapter 3. So it should be a simple enough task to work out what departments you'll need.

As an example -

Just say you're in the babycare industry. You sell prams, toys, clothes and other toddler merchandise. And just say one of your BHAGs is to deliver your goods to 1 million customers.

What are you going to need for that?

> A marketing team to generate visitors to your website

> A customer service team to handle enquiries

> A warehouse team to manage your stock.

> A delivery team of truckies or couriers.

> A finance team to manage your cash flow.

> Maybe you'll hire merchandise buyers or account managers to visit manufacturers and negotiate favourable trading terms.

See how once you think logically about your goal, a whole umbrella of supporting teams start to appear?

You don't have to get this perfect. Don't strain your brain trying to see into a future that hasn't even formed yet. Just base your chart on the information you already know.

If you've already got an org chart for your business, now's the time to revisit it. Do you have the right structure to get you towards your big 10-

year goals? Are some roles redundant? Can some roles be merged together?

Just because things have been the way they are for a long time… that doesn't mean you shouldn't challenge their relevancy and make changes when necessary.

Here's an example of what your Organizational Chart might look like:

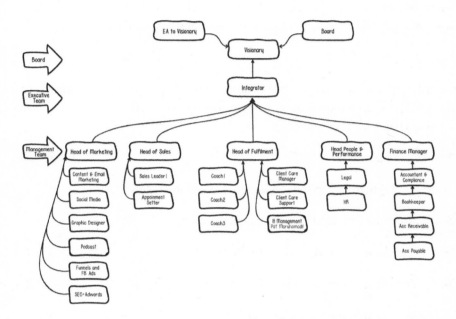

To be perfectly honest, you cannot 100% know what departments your business will need to reach your BHAGs. If you do have an idea, I guarantee it will be very different when you get there. Business is tricky like that - the further you progress, the more the landscape changes.

Your business will dictate what roles need to show up. But if nothing more right now, it's important for you to get clear on what your key departments and roles are.

You need to see the blueprint for your house. Then build it room by room.

This is how you slowly start to remove yourself from 'wearing all the hats' in your business.

As you fill each role and create fail-proof role descriptions and KPIs (I'll show you these in the next two chapters), you'll step out of each role for good.

Think back to Georgie's story at the beginning of this chapter.

After implementing a new Organizational Chart following this example, Georgie placed a few department heads who are all accountable for their own department's proper function. Now he's got just 3 direct reports, and is nearly at a point where he's ready to hire his first Integrator.

"Now I've got my CFO controlling finance - all I do is have a call with him every week to run through the key metrics of that department," he said to me during a recent phone call. "I have a head of product marketing and sales. And I have a head of partnerships. If they're doing their jobs, I know my business is on track."

"If they're hitting their KPIs, I'm happy. I don't need to worry about the other staff who work at the coalface, so to speak. They still tell me if they need my support, but that rarely happens because they're responsible for their department, not me."

Now Georgie has the time to work ON the business. Instead of scattering his time and attention between 7 different areas, he is making big strides on high-value activities that move his business towards his vision and mission.

That's what I want for you, too.

The right people in the right roles

A couple of years ago I aimed to make myself the most unreliable person in my business.

Why? Because I wanted my team to be perfectly able to do their jobs, make decisions and improve the business without me needing to advise them on every little thing.

Thanks to this (and the other principles you're learning in this book), every time I am away from the business, I come back to find it operating as good

- if not better - than when I left it.

I've got the right people, in the right roles.

If you're the bottleneck in any part of your business, not only do you slow the whole thing down, but that's also how you end up working 60+ hours a week. Because there's so much for you to do.

You don't want that. You want freedom, remember? You want your sunset.

Who are you bringing with you?

Key roles

No matter how you build your organization chart, there are three key roles that you must include if you want to structure your business so it thrives without you working 'in' it.

Visionary

The visionary is just that - the person who drives the vision of the business. A large part of the role is to keep coming up with great ideas. A great visionary has 20 innovative ideas at any one time.

The visionary role involves creativity and problem solving on a large scale. Visionaries build big relationships, lead the way with company culture, and explore new ways to keep the business thriving.

It's an emotion-based role, driven by intuition and gut instinct. The visionary typically doesn't concern themselves with smaller details - that's what their team is for. Visionaries dream big and bold.

Integrator

The integrator sits in an interesting spot in business. They are the conduit between the visionary and the key department heads. Part of their role is to filter the right information up towards the visionary, and also to lead and manage down to those in charge of each department.

It's also their job to keep all your department heads moving in the right direction (towards your WIGs, BHAGs, and ultimately up the mountain towards your sunset).

That's how you can still manage your business while hardly working in it - your integrator manages your managers, and filters *only important information* upwards. So all you need is a 25 minute chat with them to understand what's happening in every department of your business.

Department heads

Department heads lead and manage the staff within their department. These roles hold accountability for hitting KPIs, fulfilling (and improving) standard operational outcomes, as well as making sure each department stays on track with their quarterly projects.

These roles are part emotion and part strategy. A large part of the job is guiding and motivating the team to do the work required to reach each department's goals. So department heads need to show strong leadership and interpersonal skills, while also having a level head and problem-solving ability.

How to build your team easily and cost-effectively

Just because you have a lot of roles to eventually fill, doesn't mean you have to end up with an enormous team... and the frighteningly large payroll that comes with it!

Sure you can choose to hire in-house staff. But what works best for many businesses is to outsource roles - or even entire departments (such as finance or marketing).

Most of the roles on your organization chart that sit lower than the department heads can be easily taken care of by a remote team of VAs, freelancers, and other contracted service providers.

This method of team building is ideal for businesses still in the startup phase (less than $1.2 million p.a.). Because in those early days, business is more about the hustle - finding what works and getting a foothold in your marketplace.

Businesses in the startup phase don't have the time to train a team of copywriters, graphic designers, and so on. It can be far less time consuming to instead reach out to contractors or other businesses that are already experts in their own field.

You can work with them either on a per-project basis, or arrange a retainer fee for a certain amount of work each month. It's far more flexible and cost-effective.

After you start hitting 6 figure years, you may want to hire an in-house team you can train your own way. Or not. It's up to you - there are plenty of 6 and even 7 figure businesses out there that operate with just a few remote team members.

I'll cover more about managing a remote team in chapter 11.

Creating air-tight accountability in your business

An organizational chart tells you who is in what role. And the title of the role. Which is great... but that's where it ends.

But an Accountability Chart shows who's in what role, and also *what they are accountable for* in that role.

Because filling a role is just one side of the coin. Your employee doesn't just sit there (at least, they're not supposed to!) They are responsible for producing a result.

After all, your business needs to achieve outcomes. It needs action. And it needs someone to be accountable for driving that action.

This is why I believe that Accountability Charts are even more important than Organizational Charts.

An Accountability Chart shows -

What role is it
Who is in that role

What their 3-7 accountabilities are

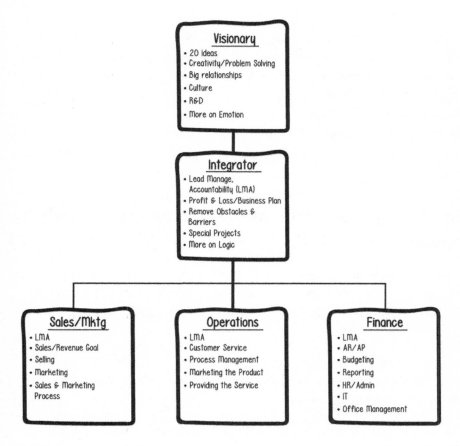

Responsibilities aren't listed in the accountability chart - they're kept in your position descriptions (that comes in the next chapter).

For now, just remember -

Accountability = responsible for an outcome

Responsibility = accountable for completing tasks

For example:

"I am a sales manager. I am accountable for my team hitting targets. But my team is responsible for the number of calls, the number of pitches, and the number of sales. I'm accountable for them hitting their target, but

they're responsible for doing the work."

Or...

"I am a project manager. I am accountable for rolling out a new sales funnel. But I have a team of 6 people who are responsible for the individual tasks within that project. It's my job to make sure things stay on track. If my team doesn't fulfill their responsibilities, it's my job to fix the problem. The team does the work, but the outcome is on me."

At The Game Changers, my managers have both accountabilities and responsibilities built into their role. I'll show you how to do that in the next chapter.

Letting your staff make decisions... within reason

When you're hiring A-players, you want them to bring their creativity, intelligence and original thought to their role. Because part of their purpose in your company is to help make it better. To innovate and improve.

In order to do that, your staff need the ability to make decisions and change processes. They need a degree of autonomy. If they need to ask you before doing anything, it results in bottlenecks and lack of innovation... both of which will cripple your business.

I'm not saying to give your staff full reign to change anything they fancy. That's a recipe for chaos. Instead, create guidelines for decision making that give your staff some freedom to just get on with their job without having to ask permission for every little thing.

My team has a bunch of guidelines they operate within that give them a large amount of autonomy within their roles.

For example -

Our marketing team can make purchases up to $250 without formal approval from their manager. Certain team members have rights to change Zapier. Others have rights to update certain systems and processes.

The type of freedoms you allow will depend on the role. Just make sure you build them into the department's operating policies - otherwise your department heads will spend all day answering little requests instead of guiding the team to hit their KPIs.

Once again, it's time for you to take *action* on what you've just learned.

Today's task is simple -

Sit down for some brainstorming time. Look at your BHAGS (big hairy audacious goals).

Reverse engineer what you think you'll need to get there. And plan it out.

Once again, use a sheet of paper or a whiteboard. You can also use my personal favorite method: Post-It notes on a window.

I get that this probably is the last thing you want to do right now. You just completed a massive section in the last chapter, when you mapped out your goals, projects, and tasks.

I know you've got a business to manage, staff to pay, sales to make, services to deliver. I get it.

You might feel like this stuff is pulling you away from what's needed.

Or what you THINK is needed.

But the reality is that if you don't put these structures in place, you're always going to stay stuck where you're at. Perpetually putting out fires. Perpetually looking at your glass ceiling but never rising above it.

And above all, you'll be perpetually tired, stressed, and having a crappy time at life when you could - and should - be living it to the fullest. Not spending every waking hour being consumed by your business.

Remember Georgie's story from earlier in this chapter? When he looks back on his life before setting up his Organization Chart, he can't believe how he used to manage so much.

"If I'd kept going like that, I think I would've gone mad," he chuckles. "I really would've flipped over the edge with all the stuff I was trying to do."

I am giving you the steps right now. I'm laying it all out. You've got worksheets. You've got resources. If you need help implementing, get in touch with The Game Changers at www.pathtofreedom.com.au/go

I've been running this framework with coaching clients and Opulence members for over 10 years, and I can absolutely promise you this -

If you put these steps into practice, you WILL build a business that works without you.

So get moving.

CASE STUDY

Profit First Accounting

When Vanessa & Edie from Profit First Accounting came on board with us they were turning over $180k a year, paying themselves $200 each a week, and working 80+ hours a week.

Sadly, that meant being largely absent from their family and friends - often even sleeping at the office!

Vanessa and Edie's tax return business model was maxed out. The only way it could grow was by throwing more volume into it... which meant more work.

So we started by helping them shift their service model away from tax returns into a recurring revenue service for business owners. Which is work they enjoyed doing far more than tax returns - a huge win for their professional satisfaction. After all, there's no point in creating a business around doing things you hate!

That's where a lot of business owners get stuck - they hold onto their current model and smash themselves into the wall trying to make it work. This is where the Inner Game (mindset) comes into it. You've got to be prepared to surrender, to let go of what you *think* you know… and be open minded to what the next stage looks like.

Vanessa and Edie took on board our suggestions and threw themselves into the unknown, trusting The Game Changers to lead the way.

They worked hard to systemize their business to operate with less staff, less overheads, and requiring less time spent 'at work'. Using the steps you're learning in this book, Vanessa and Edie literally redesigned their business, leveraging systems and technology to make it scalable, sustainable, and enjoyable.

By making a small change in their offer, and packaging their service differently, they've set themselves free with a scalable model - the sky's the limit.

After 13 months with us they're now doing $1.1Million and they'll surpass this figure in the near future too. So now they're getting incredible job satisfaction, working 3 days a week, and they've 6x'ed their business growth. Oh, and now they pay themselves FIRST, not last.

Watch their case study at: https://www.thegamechangers.com.au/edie-may-and-vanessa-fiducia-profit-first-accounting/

YOUR POSITION DESCRIPTIONS

YOUR POSITION DESCRIPTIONS

"Position descriptions do more than just communicate an opening at your company. They attract the right candidates to apply, position your business as a great place to work and ultimately help you recruit top talent quickly and efficiently."

Barry Magliarditi - The Game Changers

Your first few hires are some of the most important you'll ever make.

Because having the right people in the right roles is absolutely essential for rapid growth that's both sustainable and scalable.

And besides, you don't want your business to 'just get by' without you… you want it to grow and thrive! For that to happen, you need people. Good people.

Most business owners stuff up their first few hires. Myself included!

Maybe you've already built a team, and you're living with the consequences of some bad hires right now.

Either way, don't panic. Thanks to what you're learning in this book, you're going to start hiring A-player people who drive your business forward, even when you're not there.

We'll cover hiring in more detail in chapter 11. But first we need to understand what roles we need to hire for. And in what order.

In this chapter, you're going to:

1. Use the Task Audit™ tool to define your 'time sucks'

2. Create roles that fit your business (not the other way around)

3. Write a position description that attracts A-team players to the role

You might think position descriptions are dry and dull. That's just because you haven't been doing them right…

Done right, your position description makes these things 1000 times easier:

- Job ads and hiring

- Onboarding new staff

- Managing performance issues

Before we jump in, let's get something out of the way.

I hear so many business owners say 'there's no good people to hire out there'.

They think that their business sits in some special circle of uniqueness that makes finding the right people damn near impossible.

I've heard it all.

"My business is rural so my choices are limited."
"I can't find anybody else who can do what I do."
"My business is different so hiring is hard for us."

Frankly, it's all rubbish.

Members in The Opulence System™ regularly hire high-quality staff... despite whatever reason they once thought they couldn't. By using the position description process you're about to learn, they attract people to their business who are driven, intelligent, creative, and a great values match.

Take Jack and Jemma Ward for example.

Jack and Jemma live in rural Western Australia. They run a civil engineering business. When they first started with us, Jack believed he'd never be able to find someone else that could perform his role.

"Nobody can do it like I can Barry," he told me. "I'm going to be stuck in this position forever."

Naturally, I challenged Jack on this belief.

Actually, I challenged him so much on it during our sales conversations, that he hired me just to prove me wrong!

After Jack and Jemma signed up, the first thing we did was work on his mindset. (This is always the first thing we do with new members in The

Opulence System™).

It took about one session to dissolve Jack's limiting belief and get him to put positive energy into finding the right hire. (If you want to find out how I did it, feel free to reach out at www.pathtofreedom.com.au/go)

Then we got clear on his vision, mission, and values, which shined a light on the type of person he needed to hire.

After...

> drilling down on his BHAGs,

> doing a Task Audit (we'll cover that in this chapter), and

> working out his Organisational & Accountability Charts...

...Jack had a really clear idea of exactly who he wanted to hire, and the role he wanted them to perform.

Next Jack wrote the Position Description as you're going to do in this chapter. He laid out exactly what the job entailed, its KPIs, and what was expected of the person who took up the reins.

This Position Description became Jack's job ad. Because why reinvent the wheel?

After only 2 weeks, Jack ended up hiring someone who was willing to move to semi-rural Western Australia just to work for his company.

Jack's new hire loved the company's vision, mission and values, knew he could absolutely nail the role, and felt wholeheartedly that this job was perfect for him.

This new hire ended up becoming the Operations Manager of the business and essentially blew it up (in the good way). Which allowed Jack to step out of his operational role, and focus on high-value activities that doubled his business over the next 4 months.

You can get results like that too.

Instead of throwing out a random lure and catching all sorts of fish... a well-crafted position description throws the perfect lure to catch your dream fish. No sorting through a gazillion resumes. No trying to make someone unsuitable fit into the culture and hoping they will improve.

When you're crystal clear on the person you want, the wrong hires flip themselves out of the net, and the right ones fight for their place.

It really can be that easy.

Attracting the right people

You might be going through this book and realizing your team isn't aligned with what you want.

If that's the case, you're probably having some feelings around 'having to get rid of them'. And equally, some fear around what that looks like. Especially if you feel you 'can't find someone as good as them'.

But know this - in terms of staff, you won't attract what you *want*. You'll attract what you *are*.

Let me explain.

If you are willing to turn people away that aren't a fit for your values, and maintain your standards around what you *do* want, you'll start attracting the right people.

As the leader of your business, what you project is what you will attract. As author Richard Bach once said, 'Like attracts like.' So be clear on your values. Be clear on what you will and will not tolerate. And don't accept anything less.

Remember when we talked about energy waves back in chapter 4? We agreed that everything in the universe is electrically charged, and that the energy we project influences what we get back (like plus and minus ends on a battery).

Attracting exceptional staff is no different.

Think back to Jack and Jemma for a minute.

I knew that Jack would find the right person once he had everything in place - his vision, goals, accountability chart and so on. And once he defined his company values, he would attract the type of person he was looking for.

Because Jack got clear on exactly what he wanted, it was only a matter of time before that type of person was drawn to the job. Turns out it happened quicker than Jack ever imagined it could!

For you, it might take a few weeks, or it might happen straight away. Maybe you will stumble along the way. Maybe you'll hire someone you shouldn't because they didn't 100% match the position description, but you tried to make it work anyway.

If that happens, it's okay. Take the lesson and try again.

Because the more clearly and strongly you put that energy out there… you WILL attract the person you're looking for.

Setting your people up for success

The #1 reason staff don't succeed in your business (assuming you've hired a culture fit) is lack of clarity around their role.

If your new staff member gets random or confusing information about what's expected of them in their role, they're going to get disheartened and quit.

Joining a new company is a challenging time as it is. There's so much to learn and get your head around. Confusing the hell out of your staff by giving them no direction is a sure way to ensure a quick exit.

Position descriptions set your team members up for success. They provide an overview of what's expected. What is the purpose of this role? How does it fit into the bigger business model?

They outline the deliverables - what outputs am I required to produce? What am I accountable for in this role?

And they shine a light on the big picture. What's the vision and mission of the role? What are the values I need to live by in this role? How am I expected to show up within this company?

The good news about putting this information together is that by implementing the steps in this book, you've already done the work. You've worked out your vision, mission and values. You've set goals, projects and tasks. You've created accountabilities in the last chapter when you created your org chart and accountability chart.

Now you just need to distill that information into your position description.

Then every time you need to hire someone for the role, getting the job ad up is a 2-minute job (for your VA - not you!).

When you're onboarding a new staff member, start with their position description - the high level of exactly what they're doing, and how they're expected to do it.

And when a team member isn't performing, you can bring them back to this document and have a conversation around the parts where they're not cutting it.

No uncertainty. No guesswork. Nice and simple.

Identifying your 'time sucks'

Lots of business owners hire for roles they don't need or aren't ready for.

Before we even think of going into position descriptions, you first need to understand where you are currently spending your time.

Which tasks suck up your time the most?

Where can you be more efficient?

What should be handed to someone else?

Who do you actually need right now?

A lot of people make the mistake of thinking 'we've got too many leads, let's hire a salesperson.'

Or 'we haven't got enough leads, let's hire a marketing company.'

That can lead to a lot of money spent that didn't need to be. And also an extra layer of complexity that your business doesn't need.

We're systemizing your business so it can work without you, remember? That means no wasteful processes or people.

Here's how to identify exactly what you need most, and create a role that fits your needs perfectly. You're going to love this!

Using The Task Audit™

The Task Audit™ is the single most powerful process that I've ever used - both for my own business *and* for my clients' organizations too. It removes the guesswork for many important business decisions by providing tangible data that illuminates the best way forward.

Here's how it works -

STEP 1: RECORD

Grab a sheet of paper. A notepad. Whatever.

Record every single task you do every day, and how long it takes you to do it. Do this for two weeks.

Your task list might look something like this -

Task	Time to Complete	Frequency
Create and send invoices	15min	Daily
Produce quotes	60min	Weekly
Run daily meetings	15min	Daily
Follow up overdue invoices	30min	Weekly
Answer incoming calls	45min	Daily
Get Car Services	3hrs	Annually
Setup Facebook Ads	2hrs	Monthly
Optimise Facebook Ads	30min	Weekly

MONDAY

Check emails - 33 minutes

Follow up leads - 65 minutes

Brief team - 47 minutes

Answer staff questions - 7 minutes, 12 minutes, 16 minutes

Draft new quote - 56 minutes

Product launch meeting - 1 hour 10 minutes

Call new client - 38 minutes

Then record the frequency of which you do these things. Do you do them daily? Weekly? Hourly?

By the end of each week, compile your data into a spreadsheet that clearly identifies -

What tasks am I doing?

How long do I spend doing them?

How often do I do them?

Once you've done this for 2 weeks, you'll get a gobsmacking reality check on exactly how much time you waste doing things you barely thought were taking up your time. What's worse, many things you waste time doing don't add any value to your business.

You're ready for step 2...

STEP 2. LABEL

Look at each single task that's on your list.

It's time to squeeze the best value out of each task.

Mark each task with a D, O, C, or S -

D = **Delegate** - Can I delegate this task?

Have you already got a team member you can delegate this task to?

If you haven't got someone you can delegate the task to immediately, you could choose to do this in 2 or 3 months time. Ask 'is this task something I can train someone to take over in the near future?'

The most valuable time in your business is your own. The more time you spend on doing tasks you can train anyone to do, the less time you're spending on high level activities that bring money and growth.

For instance, I value my time at $10,000 an hour. Meaning when I have a spare hour, I can jump on a sales call, organise a joint venture, or launch a new campaign that would make me $10k.

If I can spend $50 bucks an hour on a bookkeeper, and use that hour to make $10,000 in sales... it's a no-brainer to hand over the books, right?

Take that same attitude as you go through the D.O.C.S. process. Put a dollar value on your time, and remove yourself from anything that can be done by someone else at a cheaper rate.

In chapter 9 you're going to learn how to write systems that ensure your staff perform every role to your exact standards. So if you're resisting letting go of certain tasks... it's time for a mindset check.

You cannot grow a business while still hanging on to day-to-day tasks. You are moving into the visionary role, remember? That means setting up the structure for your business to run without your daily involvement.

If you're feeling resistance during this process, look at the reasons you are *really* holding on to those tasks. What's the emotional payoff for holding on to that particular responsibility? Whatever it is, it's holding you back from growing your business.

O = Outsource - Can I pay someone else to do this for me?

I believe that when your business is in the startup phase, outsourcing is the most powerful way to grow your business.

Just say you're a tradesperson. And want to hire another tradesperson to share your workload. So you hire an apprentice.

Coming from a tradie background myself, I can tell you that apprentices do NOT make your life easier. They need you to train them in everything. That's the whole point of being an apprentice.

But it takes a long time to train someone from scratch. When you're also trying to run your business and keep up with your own workload… having an apprentice can suck the life out of you.

What if you hired a contractor instead?

Someone who already knows what they're doing, and can just get on with the job?

Yes they cost more than an apprentice. But by charging enough and factoring in the contractor's fee, you can still make far more money than by spending precious time bringing your apprentice up to speed.

You can still make money off the top of a contractor's fee. What's more important, you can trust them to do the job while you focus on growth activities for your business.

Later on when your business is running smoothly and you've got time on your hands, hire some apprentices if you like. Spend your time training them if you love developing new talent.

C = Continue - You should ONLY continue high-level activities that:

    a. you love doing, and

    b. only you can do, and

    c.   are important drivers of your business growth, and

    d.   have the highest ROI on your time.

For example, I look at my KPIs every week, because that's important for keeping my eyes on the road in my business.

I still have a weekly meeting with my integrator and get updates on recruitment, marketing, sales and so on.

I still do a 2 day planning session with The Opulence System™ members each quarter, because I'm the right person to guide this high-level activity.

I still host podcasts, because I love connecting with people and sharing value to my community. Plus they are also a high-level brand building activity.

And I dream up new ideas as the visionary, because I love coming up with cool ideas for the business and our members.

I manage high level relationships with other key players in business. I go to events. I network. I build brand value.

These are all high-level activities that are the best use of my time. They are also things only I can do to drive business growth.

S = Stop - What are you doing right now that really doesn't *need* to be done?

Think of useless activities like printing out copies of documents to be filed. Or doing things for staff members that they can do themselves. Or doing one delivery on Sunday instead of consolidating it into the week's run.

For example, Dustin and Martin are The Opulence System™ members who run a cold-pressed juice and cider company in Western Australia. When they started with us, one of the first things we did with them was look for ways to uncover hidden cashflow within their business.

As part of The Task Audit™ process, we identified that delivering products to customers over three days a week was costing them way too much, both in terms of time and money. So we asked the question: what if you stopped doing deliveries 3 days of the week?

Long story short, Dustin and Michael changed their delivery model from 3 days to 1 day a week. Which meant that they cut their delivery wages by two-thirds, and saved $150k in yearly operational costs, which meant $150,000 pure profit back in their pockets.

The best part? Their clients were still happy, and the brothers spent that extra day working ON their business... with the occasional surfing trip thrown in, because you've gotta enjoy life!

Once you really start to question all of the activities you'll see laid out in front of you, it will strike you just how much time you're wasting on stuff that you could easily cut out of your business without it affecting anything. Or at least cut down to take up far less resources.

The first time you do The Task Audit™ , you'll realise straight away there's a bunch of things you need to stop. They are things that just keep you busy. They're not moving you where you want to go.

Most people who go through this process and commit to at least the 2 weeks, they'll free up 5-10 hours a week. This becomes time they can then spend on growing their business.

To keep themselves on track, The Opulence System™ members audit their tasks every week for at least 3 months when they start shifting responsibilities within their business. I suggest you do too.

As always, we've created a handy spreadsheet you can download and fill out - get it at this link: www.pathtofreedom.com.au/resources

Getting certainty on which roles to hire for first

I don't know about you, but there are a thousand things I'd rather do than manage staff.

It's not that I don't want to help my team. I know full well that the success of my business depends on how well they do their jobs.

It's just that checking their work, following up on tasks, organizing schedules, keeping records updated and blah blah blah... even thinking about it bores me to tears.

I am happy to be the *leader* of my team. But I'm not a detail-oriented kind of guy.

Which is why I hired our amazing Integrator, Heather.

Heather loves doing the things that I hate. She is super-organized, detail-oriented, and an absolute rockstar at keeping all the pieces of my business moving as they should. She enjoys her job, and she's great at it.

But back in the day, when The Game Changers was a newbie business just getting on its feet, I did manage my team. As a business owner yourself, you know first-hand how, in the beginning, you wear all the hats.

Bookkeeper, trainer, content creator, HR dept, manager, office cleaner... at some point we've done it all.

But managing all the little minutiae of my business was something that I NEVER really enjoyed.

I'm a big picture person. I'm a leader. That's my wheelhouse.

So as soon as I was able, I hired people to take on the roles that –

1. I didn't enjoy

2. Weren't the best use of my time

Because spending hours doing something I didn't enjoy, wasn't even that great at, and didn't NEED to do was getting in the way of doing stuff that I was good at, DID enjoy, and that had better ROI on my time.

So that's why this next step of The Task Audit™ process is going to change your business forever.

STEP 3: ANALYSE

It's time to categorize your tasks into your operational departments (you completed your Organisational and Accountability Charts last chapter, remember?)

You'll likely see patterns in the types of tasks you've opted to delegate or outsource. Groups of tasks will clearly fall into one of the departmental categories within your business.

Is there a role in your Accountability Chart around the same theme as the tasks you've earmarked?

It might be office admin support. It might be a VA. It might be marketing, sales, or delivery.

That becomes your first hire.

And it tells you exactly what to write in the Position Description for the role.

Instead of copying and pasting a role from someone else's job ad (and trawling through a bunch of crappy candidates), you're essentially creating a role that fits your business perfectly. At least, for now (because you will grow and change).

If you're a bigger company with a bunch of staff already, you might get your whole team to do this task audit. Then you can compile all the data and see which tasks or roles are redundant.

Which roles can be combined to save resources?

What tasks are your staff doing that they shouldn't be?
How can priorities be shifted to be more efficient?

For example, just say you find that your sales staff are spending a few hours a week scheduling appointments. That's a task that a VA, appointment setter, or customer support team can do for them. Then your sales staff can spend more time on the phone closing clients.

The Opulence System™ members spend time during each quarterly planning session looking at their Accountability Chart, and the tasks within each role.

They ask, 'Is this still the best use of this person's time? Is it the best fit for the role, or does it need to be shifted to another role?'

Just as the roles within your business will shift and change as you grow, so will your team. Staff will outgrow their roles. So instead of having them get bored and leave, reviewing your position descriptions regularly means you can keep tweaking or recreating the roles in your company to capitalize on your team's growing skillset, and keep them happy in their role too.

Writing your position description

So far in this chapter you have -

a. Identified where you're wasting your time

b. Consolidated those tasks into a role

It's time to get to work.

Writing a position description for your new role will only take you 15 minutes. Because lucky you - you've done the hard yards in previous chapters.

Here's what to cover. And as always, we've created a free downloadable template you can fill in. Visit www.pathtofreedom.com.au/resources to get your copy.

POSITION DETAILS

Position Title:

Department:

Salary: Don't put a number here. Instead, write 'Refer to letter of offer'. I'll tell you why this is important later.

Reports To: Which department head will be in charge of managing this person's output and results? At the beginning, you may be covering this role.

Hours of work:

Review Frequency: This is important - you need to stay on top of your staff member's performance. In turn they also need to know that you will be challenging them to be at their best and be outstanding in their role, and that there will be checks and balances to ensure this happens. A-player staff aren't daunted by this - they're excited by it.

POSITION REQUIREMENTS

Purpose of position: This is kind of like the 'vision' of the role. We'll get into the detail later... for now, give your new hire a big sunset they can consistently work towards.

Accountable for: You can swipe this straight from your accountability chart. Isn't it great you've already done this work in the last chapter?

Responsibilities: Break down their accountabilities into the task-based responsibilities within their role. Once again, you don't need to go into too much detail - focus on the WHAT. We'll take care of the HOW in the next chapter (systems).

Key Performance Indicators: What are they responsible for? What benchmarks indicate their success in the role? (We'll look into KPIs next chapter.)

Recurring tasks: Write 'refer to task sheet'. The tasks within this role will change regularly as you tweak your business processes. In Chapter 10 (Automation) you'll learn how to set recurring tasks for your team.

Competencies, knowledge and experience: What do they need to know to perform their role? If they're a developer, they will need to know a few programming languages. If they're a video editor, they'll need to know their way around Adobe suite.

Desirable qualifications: This may not be applicable for every role. Your customer service team doesn't need to hold degrees. But your accounting department head certainly will.

General: This is where you write about your business. Tell them about your vision, mission and values, as well as what level of performance you expect of them.

We've covered a lot so far in this book.

You've created your ultimate vision.

You've reverse-engineered your mission, goals, and projects that will get you there.

You've identified the people you'll need to help you, and defined the structure of your company.

And now you've taken the first step in finding your first new hire to help you on your way.

In the next chapter, you'll set some benchmarks for your people's performance, and your company's performance as a whole.

Once you set these, you'll be able to monitor what's happening in your business in just a few hours a week. So you can work on your business without having to answer 50 questions a day AND knowing that your team is working optimally.

YOUR KPIS

YOUR KPIS

"Your numbers tell the story of your business. They're its signs of life, telling you where your business is bleeding, and where it is blossoming. Both are important for making strategic decisions that help you grow."

Barry Magliarditi - The Game Changers

Back in 2018, a new Tesla Model X crashed while on Autopilot mode, killing the driver.

While rightfully being sad for the person who lost their life, the world also kind of rolled its eyes. "What a surprise. The driverless car couldn't drive. Take that Musk, you smug so and so."

The National Transportation Safety Board had a meeting to determine the probable cause of the accident. It found that the driver of the car was playing video games at the time of the crash.

He wasn't looking at the road at all.

"Well, surely he didn't have to! After all, Autopilot means the car runs on, well... autopilot. Right?"

Actually, no.

Autopilot can help Tesla vehicles change lanes and maintain speed and safe distances... but it's not a completely driverless feature. Drivers still need to pay attention.

Despite Tesla making this clear to drivers, a 2019 survey found that drivers overestimate Autopilot's capabilities and get too comfortable, totally relinquishing full control over their car.

Running a business without watching your KPIs is a bit like driving a Tesla on Autopilot.

If you've got the right systems, processes, and people in place, your business *can* work without you. *But that doesn't mean you should take your eyes off the road.*

For me, even though I spend most of my year traveling, and have removed myself from the day-to-day operations of my business, I'm still paying close attention to the game.

I can look at my critical numbers and identify exactly where there's a potential problem, and forecast future problems too. I can also look at my KPIs and see where there's an opportunity to leverage even better results from something we're already doing well.

The more you track and refine your KPIs, the better you'll get at diagnosing the health of your business. And the better you can help it grow and thrive - even when you're sitting poolside in Bali like I am right now.

Unfortunately, lots of business owners have the wrong approach to their KPIs. They either don't track their critical numbers, or they track ones that aren't actually helping them grow their business.

Which is probably why they're confused and frustrated at their lack of advancement.

So in this chapter, you're going to learn:

- Exactly which KPIs you need to be tracking

- How to keep them relevant to your growth and vision

- How to use KPIs to fine-tune every aspect of your business so it runs like a racecar

This chapter is going to change the game for your business. So strap in.

But before we begin, we need to correct an error in thinking that renders most KPIs useless.

To do this, let's briefly revisit a concept introduced a couple of chapters ago...

Using a lead vs lag approach

Remember back in chapter 5 we talked about lead and lag measures?

I advised you to break down your goals into *lead measures* - things you can influence daily or weekly to ensure you reach your goals.

Your KPIs are the same.

To refresh your memory -

A lag measure is something that's already happened - you can't influence or change it.

A lead measure is something that's happening now - every day is another chance to change it.

Most business owners' KPIs are based on *lag* measures.

An example is your profit & loss report.

You might look at this monthly. Maybe just annually. When you look at your P&L, you can't influence or change those numbers. You can't go back in time and make more sales in the past.

But you can break down this lag measure into smaller *lead* measures, and influence next year's P&L.

Here's an example of what I mean:

Lag measure = I want to make $1.2 million dollars gross revenue this year

Lead measure = I need to close 10 sales per month at $10k each to earn $1.2 million this year.

So now 10 sales a month is a new KPI.

Ok. But *what needs to happen* to close 10 sales a month?

You can hire appointment setters to free up your team's time for sales conversations. You can revise your sales script to influence your conversion rate. You can rework your marketing campaigns to get better quality leads.

And you can measure your results for all of these innovations with... you guessed it! More KPIs.

Businesses like Amazon and FedEx have drilled down their KPIs so much that every *second* is measured and accounted for. Because they've got really tight delivery targets to hit. A sloppy process can have a disastrous effect on hundreds of deliveries.

For your business, KPIs might look a bit different. But once you start measuring your own critical numbers, you can truly supercharge your growth.

Because what can be measured can be improved.

Let me show you how.

From little things, big things grow

To increase your revenue and profits within your business, there are 3 main drivers:

1. Get more clients – convert more people into your service or product

2. Retain clients – increase the number of times your clients transact with you

3. Maximize spend – upsell additional products or services each transaction

But business owners usually spend way too much time focusing on #1 - leads.

I get it - cash flow is the lifeblood of business. And especially when you're just starting up, it's your primary concern.

But 'more leads' is rarely the answer to your cash flow problems.

Leads cost advertising money. They're a front-end expense.

And if your back-end systems are already broken (or non-existent!), adding more volume into the mix will only amplify the issues you're dealing with right now.

Think about it - what would happen if your business suddenly signed 50 extra clients? What would break? Delivery? Billing? Customer service? Or everything?

Instead of chasing more leads, how about improving the lifetime value of clients you already have?

Instead of throwing more volume (and money) at a cash flow problem, you can -

Improve your show up rate on sales calls.

Improve your sales closure rate.

Improve your project turnover speed.

Improve your client retention rate.
Create upsells that boost average $ per sale.

All those things (and more) add much more value to your business than just throwing more leads into the machine.

As an example, let's just say your sales KPI dashboard looks like this:

	Week 1	Week 2	Week 3	Week 4	Monthly Total
No. of Leads	20	17			
No. of appointments	10	12			
Show rate	50%	70%			
No. of sales	2	5			
Conversion rate	20%	41%			
Total Sales Value	$20,000	$68,000			
Ave Sale	$10,000	$13,600			

In terms of lead measures, you've got multiple areas you can influence to achieve the outcome you want.

Suddenly, opportunities to improve your business are everywhere.

All it takes is a marginal improvement in each tracking area to shift the needle in a major way.

Think about your total revenue right now.

What would happen if you increased your sales call booking rate by 5%?
What would happen if you increased your conversion rate by 10%?
What would happen if you increased your average sale by 15%?

These little improvements can translate into big results.

Example 1: Profit margin increase nets $36k a month

When Trent first joined us, his barbershop was doing a massive amount of haircuts every week. That meant lots of staff and lots of expenses.

Trent had some big goals - he wanted to open up more barbershops across Australia. He was also expecting his first child. So a big priority was to set up his business to provide his growing family with the life he wanted.

But Trent's big goals were limited by his cashflow. Or so he thought...

After looking at the shop's KPIs, we realized that the best cash flow strategy was to increase profit margins.

Trent's average haircut price was $31. We realized that if we took it from $31 to $39, across 1200 haircuts per week, that would add an additional $9600 per week *net profit*. No additional expenditure to the business, just simply a higher price on a service they were already offering.

Understandably, Trent was concerned that he would lose clients.

Time for some more number analysis. Thanks to his KPI tracking, we worked out that his barbershop could afford to lose 246 haircuts and still be better off. Why? Because losing 246 haircuts meant Trent could reduce his staffing overheads and save money.

And less staff meant less time managing the business, which gave Trent more time to spend on implementing new ideas to keep his customers coming back. It also meant he could spend more time with his newborn too!

In the end, the barbershop's increase from $31 to $39 only resulted in a 2% loss in weekly haircuts. Making Trent over $9k additional profit per week. That's an extra $36k a month PROFIT...

Trent grew his empire to 5 stores, and has plans to roll out more. (His kid's super cute too.)

Are you seeing how the numbers in your business can tell you everything?

Not just how it's doing *now*, but how you can *change just one measure* and rewrite the history of your business?

Let's start putting this into action.

Core KPIs to measure in your business

When The Opulence System™ members start with us, most of them don't have any KPI tracking in place. Nor do they have a clear view of what they need to be tracking.

Which is why we use The Profit Plan™.

The Profit Plan™ tracks five clear and critical KPIs that every business needs to monitor.

1. No. of leads generated

2. Conversion rate

3. No. of sales

4. Average sale value

5. Gross profit

Each of these measures influences the one below it.

For example, *number of leads* and *conversion rate* are things that you can influence to increase *number of sales*. *Number of sales* and *average sale value* influence gross profit.

There are literally hundreds of things you can do to influence each of these 'Big 5' KPIs in The Profit Plan™.

After you've implemented The Profit Plan™ and are comfortable with tracking and analyzing them, you can break them down into smaller lead measures to have even more control over our business.

But if you're new to this KPI thing, just start with The Profit Plan™.

Just doing this alone can totally change the game for your business...

We've seen clients take their conversion rate from 30% to 80%. We've seen clients go from having acquisition costs of 1000s of dollars to just a few hundred.

We've also seen clients thinking they were profitable, but realizing they were running at a near loss after they actually started tracking their numbers... just in time to save their business!

Understanding your critical numbers

In addition to The Profit Plan™, every business should track 1-3 critical numbers. These can differ a bit depending on your business model.

For example, our critical numbers are:

- **Number of active clients** (how many payers are on the books each month)
- **Retention rate** (how many clients stay with us after our 90-day 'love it or leave it' guarantee)
- **New client net gain** (how many new clients are we bringing in vs clients leaving because they've got what they need)

Your critical numbers are the vital signs of your business.

They're the 1-3 things that indicate if your business is green and growing...

or ripe and rotting.

By looking at my critical numbers, I can near-instantly check the pulse of my business, and know if it's healthy or not.

Looking at my **active clients** tells me exactly what my revenue is. Based on my revenue, I know what my gross profit is. My gross profit is fixed (we make the same profit on each member), and our overheads are fixed too… so I *instantly* know how profitable my business is at any given time.

If we're **retaining** 90%+ of members after their first 90 days, that lets me know that we're delivering phenomenal service to our clients. They're getting results, and they want to stay. And that's not just the 90-day clients, but members who have been with us for 1, 2, or even 3 years and still getting tons of value from our training, coaching, and community. That's a healthy sign of life for my business.

Because I know what our sales rates are based on active clients from the previous week, our **net client gain** lets me know we're generating the right amount of leads, making the right amount of sales, and keeping the right amount of clients past 12 months.

So although your critical numbers may not look super deep at first glance, they show you whether your business is moving in the right direction, or if something is off.

And if something's off, they show you where to look to find the problem.

Because the type of problem indicates which department needs attention.

Remember the fundamental business areas we covered in chapter 5?

> Marketing
> Sales
> Fulfillment
> People performance
> Financials

Whatever measure is lagging in your KPIs shows you exactly which department to troubleshoot.

Applying this to The Profit Plan™, you've got -

No. of leads generated - that's marketing

Conversion rate - that's sales

No of sales - that's sales again

Average sale value - that's marketing + fulfillment

Gross profit - that's financials

KPIs tell you exactly where your business is bleeding, and where it is blossoming. Both are important for making strategic decisions that help you grow.

How to identify your core KPIs

If you've never tracked KPIs in your business before, now's the time to get started. And if you have been tracking them in your business, it's a good idea to revisit them and make sure you're using your data optimally.

If you're just starting out, start with The Profit Plan™.

Look at your numbers and identify the low performers. Start to innovate there.

For example, if you've got a leads issue, you can ask -

- What determines the number of leads?

- What can I influence to change this number?

For instance, just say you've got a budget of $100 a week and you spend $10 per lead. That's 10 leads per week.

What would happen if you could get your cost per lead down? What if you could get cheaper clicks? By looking at this metric, and making improvements that get your lead cost down to $5 per lead, that's an extra

10 leads per week.

The more you track your KPIs over time, the more patterns will start to appear. Questions to ask yourself are -

Where is the biggest hole in the numbers?

Which numbers are the most inconsistent?

Which areas are easiest to innovate for the most yield?

A lot of our clients come to us believing they have a leads problem. Where in fact they actually have a conversion problem, an average sale problem, a lifetime value problem, or a profitability problem.

Leads are often the last thing we focus on. Because leads cost money. If there are other holes in the bucket, for instance the conversion rate or average sale sucks... we're wasting money on leads that could be spent on equipment upgrades, innovation, marketing, and so on.

Example 2: Leads increase yields $12,000 in sales

When Jacob approached The Game Changers, he was trying to get his gym off the ground. But he was $300k in debt.

Jacob had been desperately trying to get new leads, but every investment he made into marketing failed to produce the results he wanted. He was hemorrhaging money - to the point where his own employees were investing in the business to keep it afloat.

Needless to say, Jacob was earning no wage. He was unable to support his partner or pursue his lifestyle dreams.

During our coaching, we identified that Jacob's best opportunity was to bring more leads in. But we showed him how to do it differently. Although Facebook advertising hadn't worked for Jacob before, it was his best platform for reaching his local audience. What he really needed was to hone his niche and his offer.

After working with Jacob to get crystal clear on who he was targeting, and helping him create a *can't-say-no* offer to lure them in, Jacob earmarked $600 for ad spend, and built a new ad campaign. Thanks to his new message-to-market match, the campaign took off and resulted in over $12,000 in sales.

Jacob's member numbers grew by over 130% in the first three weeks of launching his new ad campaign. Soon Jacob's kids' programs were filled months in advance. Finally Jacob was making a profit to reinvest back into the business.

He expanded his team, systemized his business using the principles you're learning in this book, and started working from home 2 days a week. And he welcomed his first child! (We can't take credit for helping with that part!)

Choosing your KPIs

Lots of people put KPIs on their dashboard just because they think they should. But every KPI should earn its place on the board by providing you with valuable information about how you're tracking, and what you need to change and improve.

There are hundreds of things you can measure. But that doesn't mean that you *should*.

It's important to question <u>why</u> you're measuring each KPI. How does it contribute to the health of your business and its systems?

As the business visionary, you personally only need to monitor your critical numbers and other important high-level KPIs. Each department might have 10-20 KPIs they measure - but this detail doesn't need to come to you. It's for your department heads and integrator to monitor.

For example, my marketing department measures ad reach and impressions and a bunch of other details. These influence the critical numbers I track from my marketing department:

> cost per lead,

> number of leads, and
> cost per appointment

If those numbers are off, I go to my Integrator who liaises with the marketing department head who creates the changes needed to get things back on track.

As another example, in sales, we measure -

No of dials

No of appointment settings

Connection percentage

No of triages booked per connection

Booking vs connection percentage rate
And a whole lot of other stuff...

These numbers tell us the volume of leads, the quality of leads, how our individual appointment setters are working, how our systems work to get people to show up to the call...

The data gives me so much information on how my business is operating, without me having to set foot in the office.

I run through my KPI dashboard on a 15-minute Zoom call with my Integrator on a Monday morning. In seconds I can see if there's an issue, and if there is, I can also see where we need to focus to fix it.

Think about your KPIs this way.

To continue with the car analogy from earlier, you measure the revs, you measure the speed, the temperature, and the fuel. Just like the 5 KPIs in The Profit Plan™, those measures form the basis of telling you how your vehicle is operating.

The temperature is too hot. The fuel's a bit down. I'm speeding. Why is my car revving so much, do I need to change gears?
The Profit Plan™ lets you drive your business successfully... keeping your eyes on your vehicle AND the road ahead.

After you're comfortably using The Profit Plan™ KPIs, you can start to build out your dashboard. What other elements have you identified that directly influence your business growth and progression towards your vision?

Remember that every KPI has to mean something. You don't just add gauges on your car for the sake of it, do you? There has to be a reason why you're measuring every KPI. And you have to know how to influence it. Otherwise there's no point.

When you're ready to start tracking more KPIs, stop and look at your business strategically.

'What is the biggest problem in my business right now?'

Is it culture?

Is it a struggle with cash flow?

Is it that we've got heaps of leads coming in but no sales?

Is it that we have no leads coming in and sales staff are just sitting around?

And then, reverse engineer the problem by saying 'ok where's the actual root cause?'

For instance, just say your problem is that you're not making any sales.

Is it because you haven't got leads?

Or is it because your sales conversion sucks?

Or because your sales staff aren't doing their job?

Spend time getting super clear on your problem's origin - where does it begin?

Once you know what's fuelling the problem, put a KPI on it. Track it. Measure it. And innovate within your business to improve it.

What can be measured, can be improved.

Expanding on your KPIs

Eventually, you want to be constantly tracking 5-7 KPIs in each department. Maybe more.

For example in your marketing department, your KPIs might look like this -

- no. of leads
- cost per lead
- cost per appointment
- cost per acquisition
- cost per click

In sales, if you're doing cold calling you might measure -

- number of dials vs connections
- connections vs calls booked
- number of appointments scheduled
- number of sales
- conversion rate

In fulfillment, you might be measuring -

- no. of hours spent delivering a service vs quoted estimate
- turnaround time from order placed to delivery
- quality control vs speed of delivery
- customer satisfaction and follow up

Financially you might measure things like -

- Gross profit
- Net profit
- Monthly collectibles
- Aged receivables under 30 days
- Aged receivables over 30 days

And so on.

I get that each business is different. If you want to discuss which KPIs you should be tracking, and get some strategic ideas on how to influence them, please feel free to reach out to The Game Changers at www.pathtofreedom.com.au/go

Example 3: Average sale value increase nets $1.4 million

When Chris and Jeff joined The Game Changers, their auto parts retail business had been on a 10% downtrend in sales for 2 years. They were losing $1.3 million dollars a year.

Not surprisingly, their cash flow was tight, and they were afraid of losing their company. It was impacting them personally too - that much stress and pressure is sure to affect all your relationships, not just business ones!

At first, Chris and Jeff were resistant to spend money on coaching. Having a physical store, they needed instead to keep products on the shelves. Or so they thought...

During their Game Plan™ session, we realized that if we grew their *average sale* to $22 across the board, over the 59k transactions they had per year it would equate to $1.298 million dollars.

So we worked on helping them increase their average sale value. This involved multi-purchase incentives, upsells, negotiating value buys with suppliers, and a number of other strategies.

The end result?

We actually increase their average sale to $29. This resulted in $1.4 million dollars in growth for Chris and Jeff.

Just from that ONE improvement, we were able to help these guys completely turn their business around. Now they have more time to focus on areas of their business that they'd been neglecting for years.

Their stress levels are normalized too, and for the first time in a long time, they're excited about their business again. That's how powerful The Profit Plan™ is.

Bottom line -

Everybody thinks that they need a new fancy marketing funnel. They think that if you just pour more leads into their system, everything will be rosy.

But if you're pouring leads into a poorly performing (or downright broken) system, then you're just going to have the same problems multiplied.

Instead of filling a leaky bucket, look for the holes in your results and use the Profit Plan™ to reverse-engineer better outcomes.

There are hundreds of ways to improve your KPI results in every department. If you're stuck for ideas, we've created a free resource that includes 346 strategies to influence all 5 core KPIs in The Profit Plan™.

Download it for free at www.pathtofreedom.com.au/resources

Creating your KPI dashboard

There are a lot of ways you can create your KPI dashboards. Quite a few fancy software solutions will give you loads of pretty graphics and all the bells and whistles.

But don't overcomplicate things - updating and tracking your KPIs shouldn't become another chore that takes up your time and doesn't add value in your business.

For us at The Game Changers, we use a shared Google Spreadsheet.

If you're a bells-and-whistles kind of person, go and make something fancy if you wish. But I advise that as with most things in life, keeping it simple is the best way to go.

Make sure you have 3 targets for each KPI:

- In progress

- Below target

- Above target

Use a traffic light system to qualify each data set.

Above target (>85%) = green
In progress (>65%) = yellow
Below target (<45%) = red

That gives you a really clear and quick visual of how you're tracking. Use conditional formatting to add colors to your last column. As you move through the quarter, you'll see KPIs turning green.

The traffic light system gives your team a sense of winning all the time, because they can see things turning green and improving. Which is great for motivation and job satisfaction. Simple and effective!

Establishing your tracking frequency

If you're focusing on lag measures and looking at your Profit and Loss report in December, that means you've only got one time each year to make critical changes that move your business forwards. Obviously, this is a pretty bad way to run a business. And you won't survive for long.

Your business needs to be agile. It needs to be able to make tiny changes to your *lead measure* KPIs to influence the big *lag measure* at the end of the year.

If you're tracking KPIs weekly, that means that you've got 52 opportunities a year to make incremental changes that steer you closer to your goals and ultimate vision.

With that in mind, you should be looking at your KPIs every week. Your departments should be tracking those numbers every day. *Did we hit enough sales calls today? What can we do to stay on target tomorrow?*

Make your KPIs part of your weekly meetings. Make them a part of your department heads' daily conversations with staff.

The grand idea is that KPI data will flow up from your staff to your department heads daily. Which then flows up from department heads to your Integrator weekly. And the critical numbers then flow up from your Integrator to you, the Visionary.

Keeping your KPIs relevant

At The Game Changers, we set our KPIs on a quarterly basis. We guide our The Opulence System™ members to do the same.

Because when you review your KPIs, you may realize that some of them aren't actually relevant. And some others might pop up occasionally that you realize you need to add.

Business is fluid - it's constantly changing and evolving. So keeping tabs on your KPIs in quarterly reviews helps you stay tightly in control of the key measures that drive the health and success of your business.

Quarterly KPI tracking aligns with your quarterly business planning too. And setting quarterly dashboards also means that if you can change and add things without screwing up a whole year's worth of data (I learned that lesson the hard way!)

Each quarter, go through your KPIs one-by-one and ask:

- Did this impact our business?

- How did this measure help us grow?

Then remove anything that wasn't useful, and add other metrics that are of value. That ensures that you keep measuring the right things to stay on track for achieving your mission and vision.

Before you go

By now you're probably itching to set up your KPIs (or improve them if you're already tracking things). But don't go away and create a massive spreadsheet with 50 KPIs all at once.

Especially if you're new to this, start with The Profit Plan™ and get used to it, get your team used to working with it, and then just add one or two more KPIs at a time.

Otherwise your KPIs will just become another task that doesn't add value to your business - which is exactly the OPPOSITE of their purpose!

If you want to get started quickly and easily (of course you do), we've created a sample dashboard you can download for free at this link -> www.pathtofreedom.com.au/resources

SYSTEMS

SYSTEMS

"Before I started systemizing my business, I was doing a whole bunch of stuff just to keep the wheels on. Now I'm actually driving the car. I'm not controlled by my business anymore. Instead, I control my contribution to the business."

Tom Cross - Cross Coastal Carpentry and Construction

"Is that your baby?"

Last year, I jumped back on the phones again for a couple of weeks. Simply because I love sales, and I felt like doing it. Just because your business operates without you doesn't mean you have to stop doing work you enjoy!

Anyway, on this particular afternoon, I was on a sales call with a guy named Tom. And I could hear a baby crying in the background.

"Yes, she's just 6 months old," Tom told me. "She's the main reason I reached out to you."

"How so?"

"I just know I've gotta do something about where I'm going. I don't want to go back to a job. I want to give my daughter a better life, and have the freedom to be around as she grows up."

"Why don't you have that freedom now?" I felt I knew the answer… but I had to ask.

"My day starts at 5am. I'm straight out of the house and at a job site before my wife and baby are even awake. I get back just before dinner. Then after dinner I jump on the computer for a few hours to catch up on paperwork. On Sundays I spend 4-8 hours just prepping for the week ahead."

"Sounds like not much of a life, Tom."

"It's not. When I can grab some time to spend with my wife, I can barely stay awake because I'm always so tired."

Tom runs a construction business that focuses on repairs for insurance companies.

Some weeks things would be really hectic. Tom and his team would be run off their feet, and work super long days. Then other weeks they'd have nothing on and Tom would be worrying about paying his team.

It made it impossible to plan anything for his business - he didn't know when cash would come in. So he hustled. Hard.

Through sheer force of will, Tom grew his business. But it relied completely on him. If he took more than 2 days off, everything fell apart. Like most business owners, Tom was good at what he did, but he'd never been taught how to run a sustainable business.

His team was working hard and making money, but Tom felt he was peddling like hell but getting nowhere. His life felt utterly chaotic.

After joining The Opulence System™, Tom set to systemizing his business to give him back his most precious resource: time.

Using the Task Audit™ and the 'System for Writing Systems™' (you'll learn that in this chapter), Tom trained his VA to start systemizing the tasks he wanted to give away.

As I was writing this book, I caught up with Tom to check in on how life looks now.

"I've got back control," Tom tells me. "I turn off on Friday night, and turn back on Monday morning. I get home at 4pm every day to spend time with my family. And there's no more weekend work."

"How's the business going?"

Tom laughs. "You could say it's pretty good... we've tripled in size and I'm finally off the tools. I've got systems in place now for running all the day-to-day stuff in my business. I really feel like I'm in the driver's seat now. Things are looking good."

"That's so awesome dude."

It's been said that doing the same thing over and over and expecting a different result is madness.

I'd say that doing something over and over and getting the *same* result is the trademark of an optimized system.

Systems are the most important element of building a business that scales and thrives without you.

Without them, your staff remain highly reliant on you. So you stay stuck in your business, fielding endless questions, putting out regular spot-fires, and spending your time training new hires.

When everything relies on you to run smoothly, there's no capacity to grow. Because although you may work with superhuman dedication, your daily output is still limited. We're only capable of so much.

What's worse, ad hoc training and rules turn any business into a circus - and the more players in the ring, the more chaotic things get.

Lack of clarity breeds inefficiencies, which in turn leads to wasted time, inconsistencies delivered across the board, and fed-up staff who get sick of the chaos and leave.

All of these problems cost your business money.

If you're currently the ringleader of a non-systemized business, it's probably costing you a bit of your sanity, too.

Bottom line - doing a repeatable task yourself more than once is the ultimate time sinkhole.

And you've got bigger things to focus on.

Since you've been following this book, by now you've got a bunch of goals to hit, projects to deliver, positions to hire for, and KPIs to track.

You're probably thinking, "I don't have time to create systems for everything!"

And you're right. Which is why in this chapter I'm going to show you how to create ONE system, and have your team create the rest. *Without* making a huge mess of it or compromising on quality.

My system for creating systems is an airtight method for ensuring that efficiency, quality of service, and profitability are maximized, tracked, and habitually improved.

Think about it - your business is made up of *hundreds* of systems. You have a system for onboarding new clients. A system for collecting payments. A system for opening the showroom in the morning. A system for hiring new staff.

Even if you don't have these things documented right now, somebody still does them regularly (to varying levels of success).

Systems show your staff how to achieve a predictable outcome for every repeatable task in your business. They remove the guesswork and turn every process into something that can be measured and improved.

The beautiful thing about having systems in place is that whenever there's a problem, the first question to ask is: *Was the system followed?*

Then it's a simple yes / no decision tree scenario to identify and fix the problem.

If the system wasn't followed, why? What needs to change for this not to happen again?

If the system was followed, what went wrong? What needs to change for a better outcome?

Using the method I'm about to teach you, each system becomes a process of constant ongoing improvement. Instead of having no idea about what's going wrong in your business, or not knowing where to start to make changes, your systems will highlight exactly where the leaks are.

At The Game Changers, we have a documented system for everything. We even have a system for reviewing systems.

Systemizing this way has helped us scale to multiple 7 figures and grow a tribe of very happy clients, even though our team is relatively small and all work remotely. It's also helped our clients achieve 2x, 4x, and even 5x growth within 6-12 months while actually scaling back their workload.

It's time to turn your business into a well-oiled machine with steps in place to ensure consistency for your clients. Because…

Consistency is king

In October 1948, the McDonalds brothers were struggling to make their restaurants profitable. A large menu meant long cooking times, inefficient kitchens, and lots of food wastage.

Then came their billion-dollar idea...

'What if we could streamline their kitchens to produce a limited menu more efficiently?'

By implementing systems in their restaurants' food production line, the McDonald brothers started producing cheap food at speeds and in quantities never heard of before.

Everybody loved the concept of this new "fast food". But it wasn't just the 'fast' bit that people loved about McDonald's.

The other side of the coin was a much more powerful thing than speed: *consistency*.

McDonald's systems meant that the same product was produced, to the same quality, every time. Even today, you can go into a McDonald's in Melbourne or Shanghai and get the same quality of chip or burger.

Consistency builds trust.

Trust is the #1 non-negotiable ingredient for building a strong brand and business. Sales simply do not happen without the buyer having a good level of trust in the seller.

On the flip side, inconsistency chips away at trust. (See what I did there... flip… chips…)

If you walked into any independently owned burger joint, you'd be rolling the dice on quality. Maybe your burger would be really greasy. Maybe there would be too much cheese. Maybe the beef patty would taste a bit funky.

You might waste your ten bucks on a less than enjoyable experience.

Most people will choose to repeat a previous pleasant experience rather than take a chance on a new unknown one. That's because *certainty* is a core driver behind human behavior.

Sure, we do like a bit of variety from time to time (some of us more than others). But as a whole, people don't like taking chances too often, especially in stressful times. They want something they can count on.

With that in mind, think about this.

If your clients get a different level of service every time they deal with your business, how are they going to feel?

What would happen if a project runs smoothly one week, and the next it's bungled at every step? What if one week your staff are super-responsive to messages, and the next week they ignore all client requests? What if one customer service agent tells your client one thing, and another tells them conflicting information?

In every scenario, that customer is going to feel uncertain about doing business with you pretty damn fast.

Systems allow your quality of service to be upheld and delivered at scale. When you have systems in place, it doesn't matter if you have 5 or 50 clients on the books - everyone gets the same quality that benchmarks your standard of excellence.

Before we dive into creating them, you must first understand the parts of a successful system.

Systems, processes, and how-tos

This powerful trio enable your business to run efficiently no matter how many staff, clients or products you've got.

Similarly to goals, KPIs, your organization chart, and everything else we've covered so far in this book, these three elements work in a top-down structure. Meaning they start with the big picture, and drill down into more detailed chunks of information.

A system is a set of things that work together to achieve an outcome in your business. Just like a railway system is a network of trains, tracks, and personnel each system in your business may contain a group of processes, instructions, templates, and checklists.

A process is the steps within a system that must be followed in order to achieve a successful result. Think of a process as a map of the pieces within each system. We like to use flow charts to visually map the actions and decisions that move us through each system.

Here's a look at one of our process flow-charts -

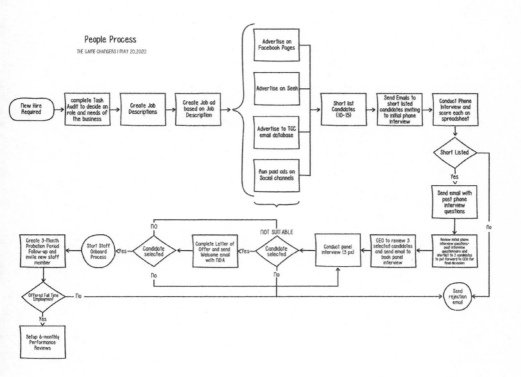

How-tos are step-by-step detailed instructions that outline exactly how to perform the steps within a process. How-tos detail the task at hand, why it's important, who's responsible, where information is, when it's done, and how it's done. And most importantly, they document what a successful result looks like.

Each how-to might consist of a document, it might include a template, or a decision-making matrix... whatever an employee needs to perform that step of the process flawlessly.

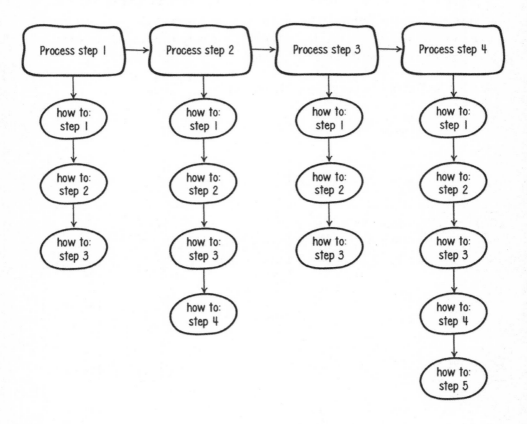

The end goal here is that you have a system, process flow chart, and supporting how-to documents for every outcome that you want to achieve in your business.

When this is set up correctly, your business is truly a self-sustaining machine. No one staff member is a single point of failure.

If Brett from marketing comes down with the flu, Penny can easily pick up the reins while he's away. If Sharon from accounting elopes to Vegas, you can have a new hire performing the role just like Sharon did in less than a day.

Remember this: Information is *everything*, and how well it's organized in your business directly influences your quality of operations.

How to create systems in your business

Here's how we create systems that ensure a business runs smoothly.

1. Map out every step within a process.
If you loved using a sticky-note scrum board for organizing goals and KPIs, you're going to really love mapping out your systems.

Grab your pack of Post-Its and clear a window or whiteboard - this is your new workspace. Pick a system to optimize (in a minute I'll show you which to do first). Then brainstorm every step involved in getting from Point A to Point Z within that system.

For example, just say you're systemizing client onboarding. What needs to happen in the client's journey to set them up for success?

At The Game Changers, new clients need to -

Sign their contract

Receive a welcome call

Set up payments

Be introduced to the online members' group

Get sent a welcome pack

Receive our onboarding email series

Schedule their Game Plan™ coaching session
And so on...

Write down every single thing on your sticky notes, and arrange them in order.

Then it's time to build fail switches into your process. After all, some steps might not work on the first few runs. Others might get missed. How can you ensure that everything within your process happens as it's supposed to?

Simple *yes / no* or *if / then* devices work best.

Once we've got that map done on the whiteboard, take a photo and send it off to a VA to put it into a flowchart.

Here's an example of how we do it:

The Process for Implementing a System
BARRY I MAY 20,2020

2. Have your team write a system for the process.

As I said earlier, you shouldn't be writing every system in your business.

Especially considering you're not the expert at everything - that's what you've hired staff for! So let them write their own system and take charge of their role.

To guide them, shoot a quick video outlining what the process is, how it fits into the larger picture of your business, and what its outcome should look like.

Give the video to a team member to write a system for what you've just outlined using the 'system for writing systems' (I'll cover this in a minute).

When the system is done, let your employee run through the process within it a few times, and have someone check their work until you are 100% confident in them. Then, hand it over - it is now their responsibility to maintain and improve the system.

**If you're the type of person who prefers working backward to reverse-engineer things, just flip this order - do the how-tos first, then collate them into a flow chart.*

3. Execute the system, measure its results, and schedule reviews.

Before execution, make sure each system document gets reviewed by management to make sure that it covers everything. It then gets named properly and added to your document registry. (I'll talk about the document registry a bit later.)

Then it's time to roll it out. Put KPIs on the measurable parts of the system. After the system is first rolled out, check these KPIs daily. Are things going to plan? Or is something being missed? Adjust as necessary.

Do this until you trust the system works. But don't take your eyes completely off the road... schedule some checks and measures to ensure the system is still operating functionally. (Your quarterly business planning is a great time to schedule system reviews.)

I'll go into this in more detail next chapter.

The system for writing systems

Right now your mind may be spiraling with a flood of documents, flow charts, and the like. And it probably seems like a lot of work.

As I have said before, it is a lot of work. But for someone else - not for you.

A lot of business owners believe they need to be the ones to create all the processes and systems. This belief slowly buries them under a growing avalanche of half-finished documents.

In actual fact, there are only two documents that you personally need to create:

1. A system for creating systems.
2. A process for automating systems.

We'll cover number 2 in the next chapter: automation.

For now, let's look deeper at how to create a system for writing systems. Get this right, and you'll only have to write that ONE document and your staff will do the rest.

The best part? They'll do it to your standards. Because the way we do this covers *everything* they need to do a stellar job.

Here's what your 'system for writing systems' document must cover. When it's complete, it serves as the template for all other systems within your business.

Purpose

At the beginning of this book, when we first started building the framework for systemizing your business to run without you, we started with *vision*. In other words, your ultimate purpose. Your vision is the overarching reason for doing what you do.

Similarly, every systems document in your business MUST start off with *purpose*.

What's the bigger picture? What's the outcome we're trying to achieve?

Then we drill down...

Why is this important?

This section is for orienting the person responsible for executing this task within the broader picture of your business. How is this relevant to the business mission and goals?

Who

Who is responsible for executing this task?

What role does this task fall under?

Hyperlink the position description you wrote in chapter 7 to provide extra clarity.

When

What's the frequency of this? When is it rolled out?

How

This section is for detailing the steps required to perform the system. We hyperlink videos, the process map, and every relevant how-to document so that someone can follow the entire system from end-to-end.

For example:

Step 1: Watch this explainer video
Step 2: Review the process map
Step 3: Complete the how-to document for this step
Step 4: Complete the how-to document for this step
Step 5: The next step
… and so on.

Including an explainer video at the start of all your 'how' sections is important. Because people have different preferred learning styles. Some people read your documents and that's enough. Others will need to watch it being explained or demonstrated.

It doesn't matter whether you're a plumber installing a tap, or a coach explaining how to deal with a client problem. If you record a quick video of how to do both properly, it eliminates many mistakes.

What done looks like

As I just mentioned, everyone processes information differently. Some people are very visual. Some people are kinaesthetic. Some people are digital.

So although you've outlined the steps in as much detail as possible, it's still important to give an example of what a good outcome looks like.

You might put a screenshot of an ad, a hyperlinked blog post example, a photo of the completed job, or whatever you can use to clearly communicate the desired result.

Checklist

By the time someone's done this process a few times, they don't need to read every detail anymore. So rather than making them waste time going through the document again and again, we include a checklist here that they can jump through quickly while still making sure they don't miss a step.

Review / if you have a problem

When is this system being reviewed - annually? Bi-annually? Quarterly?

And what happens if something's unclear, or if things are looking screwy as someone's working through this document? Who to contact?

Hyperlink the email address of the correct person to go to for help.

That's it!

If you'd like a template of this system, we've created one for you. Download it for free at this link: www.pathtofreedom.com.au/resources

I'm sure you're seeing how powerful this is.

The great thing is how simple it is to learn, and how easy it is to roll out.

Every time you bring on a staff member, make sure that teaching them this system for writing systems is in their orientation package.

That way, your team are empowered with the knowledge to roll this out whenever required. Which means that essentially every time your team get taught something, or do something new, they know how to create a system around it. So nobody wastes time figuring out how to do the thing from scratch again.

If I need a new process in my business, I simply shoot a quick Loom video explaining what I want to happen, send it to my amazing VA, and she creates the whole system for me and assigns responsibility to a team member in our team management portal Asana. (We'll cover this in a later chapter.)

Thanks to the structure I've just outlined, that team member has everything they need to execute the system with virtually no training required.

Create your system for writing systems. Train the people to use it. It's really that simple.

Which systems to create first

Regardless of what business you're in - whether you're selling coaching, or you're in a trade business, you own a gym, or whatever else - there are between **four to eight core systems** that power your organization.

Similarly to the core departments within your business, these make up the base of a functioning, systemized business.

For example, at The Game Changers our core systems are:

1. **Strategy and execution:** How we go about strategically planning innovation, and executing project plans.
2. **Our marketing system:** How we go about attracting prospects right through to taking the first step in our sales process.
3. **Our sales system:** This covers from when they opt-in,

all the way through our sales funnels, to where they either are marked as lost or become a client.

4. **Our onboarding journey**: How we set up what our coaches and support staff do to orient new members in the program and get them started on the right foot.

5. **Our people system:** How we go about finding, hiring, and managing staff.

6. **Financials:** Our system is divided into three parts: accounts payable, accounts receivable, and investment and debt management.

7. **System management:** How we manage systems within the business.

Your business might look a little different. But I'm betting if you break it down, you have 4-8 core processes that run your engine, so to speak.

To define where to start systemizing (or updating the systems you already have), there are a few ways you can approach things.

Method 1: Start with 'The Money Map'

The money map is essentially everything involving lead attraction, through to conversion, through to fulfillment.

In other words, the things that drive income for your business.

Nine times out of ten, most businesses will start here. Once you systemize the money map, then you've got working systems that support your cash flow. So you can focus on other areas.

Method 2: Look for the bleed

Look at the core departments in your business. Look at your KPIs (if you have been tracking them before now).

Where are the bottlenecks?

Which department is the biggest mess?

Where is your business bleeding time or money (or both)?

I don't know the story of your business, so you could be churning through staff, or your delivery to clients, or your financial management, or you might owe a bucketload of debt.

Any of these is a good indicator. Start there.

Method 3: Use The Task Audit™

Remember in chapter 5 we used the Task Audit™ to set our goals?

If things feel really chaotic, it's time to revisit this powerful tool.

Use the Task Audit™ to work out which tasks cost you the most amount of time or money. Get your staff to track their time for 2 weeks to highlight inefficiencies in their schedules too.

Look for the gaps and opportunities.

Is there a pattern? Do they all fall into the same department?

When you see the pattern, you know where to start. If you don't see a pattern, color-code your spreadsheets by giving each task a 'current level of efficiency'. Use the traffic light system to highlight tasks red, yellow, or green.

Then count the red tasks by department. The department with the most red tasks gets systemized first. Simple!

Controlling information flow between departments

The more efficiently information flows within your business, the better the business will run. Information roadblocks and inconsistencies hold up your staff from doing their jobs.

Which is why it's paramount to use a robust cloud filing structure - especially if you run a remote team like I do.

At first glance, file administration may seem like a pretty boring subject. But mislabelled files, lost documents, and information black holes cost businesses millions of dollars each year in wasted time, inefficient operations, and lost knowledge.

Anyone who has ever looked for a document without knowing the file name can attest to the enormous amount of time that gets wasted trawling through an internal file 'system' that follows the logic of a Mad Hatter tea party.

If you're lost in a digital sinkhole filled with documents labeled at random, such as '*merch ideas for March*' or worse, '*visitor stats 2014 final V2 final FINAL* '... it's about time you set some clear parameters and unravel the mess.

Setting up your information filing structure

At The Game Changers, our Organization Chart dictates the structure of our internal files and folders. We have a folder for our core operational files, a folder for marketing, a folder for people performance, and so on.

All this is kept in a central cloud location. We use Google Drive, but there are a number of software options that can serve as a central knowledge hub. Staff members have *read, write* or *edit* access depending on the accountabilities and responsibilities within their role.

Most importantly - and you'll see why in later chapters - we have a separate folder for systems and processes. There are 2 main reasons for this.

1 - Ease of access.

Systems and processes documents allow your team to operate your business for you. So they need to be accessed easily from a central place where everyone knows where they are.

New team members who aren't aware that there's an Operational Process document outlining their role in *E drive/march 2019/ B.1.2.5* (or whatever) won't know how to perform their job properly. They'll just make it up as they go along. And that costs you money however you look at it.

2 - Security.

When you have all your system and process files stored in a central location, you can lock that baby down so that nobody can alter those files EXCEPT for the person in charge of that system.

If you allow team members to make changes to your systems documents, you're going to end up with trouble as, once again, your files suffer from the Frankenstein effect. If everyone can chop and change processes, that means essential steps can be edited out, resulting in all sorts of trouble.

So keep your file structure like this:

1. CORE / OPERATIONS

2. MARKETING

3. SALES

4. DELIVERY / FULFILMENT

5. PEOPLE / HR

6. FINANCES

7. **SYSTEMS AND PROCESSES**

Restricting your *systems and processes* folder to 'read access only' means that your team can't change things without going through your document management process first.

Team members in each department can add and edit files in their own folders as they see fit. But only give each department READ access to your systems and processes files. Excepting of course, the ONE person who is in charge of maintaining each system.

Why make just one person accountable?

Because any time more than one person is accountable for a task, it diffuses that sense of accountability.

People take a step back. 'Oh, I thought Karen was doing that'. It creates finger-pointing. And it creates jumbled communication - or worse, no communication at all.

The Document Registry

The Document Registry is a crucial element of your internal communications strategy. Because the more complex your business gets, the more documents you're going to create (and your staff will too). With no structure, it's pretty easy to start drowning in obsolete files, lost connections, and misinformation.

For instance, your new hire is working off your sales process version 1.4 instead of 1.5. Your marketing team is wasting time creating new process documents for things that already exist. Your sales guy is using the wrong contract.

Messy information means mistakes. And it means wastage.

I hate wastage. I'm sure you do too. So pay attention to this section.

Your document registry is a spreadsheet that lists all the core system files in your business. In terms of your internal information structure, it's kept in your Systems folder. Each document is listed in numerical order for each department, and is hyperlinked to its live file.

Here's what ours looks like -

Systems & Processes Document Registry

	A	B	C	D	E	F	G
1	7 CORE PROCESSES	Document Number	REV	Document Number	Title	File Type	Date Approved
2	PRO-01 - TGC HEART						
3							
4	THE HEART	FLO-001-001		Flowchart	How to Implement New Process with TGC		
5		PRO-001-001		Process	System for Writing Systems	Word	
6		PRO-001-002		Process	Communication Rhythm		
7		PRO-001-003		Process	The Power Process		
8		PRO-001-004		Process	Email and Calendar Management Process for the CEO of The Game Changers		
9							
10	Product Development	FLO-001-002		Flowchart	Process for Implementing Systems		
11							
12							
13	PRO-02 - MARKETING						
14	Content Creation and distribution			Flowchart	Content Creation & Distribution		
15	Active Lead generation			Flowchart	Active Lead Generation		
16	Facebook Ads Funnel	FLO-002-001		Flowchart	TGC Facebook Ads Funnel		
17		FLO-002-002		Flowchart	Podcast Execution Flowchart-Libsyn Uploading		
18		FLO 002 003		Flowchart	Podcast Execution Flowchart		
19		FLO-002-004		Flowchart	Make It Rain		
20							
21		PRO-002-001		Process	Download Edited Podcast and Create Content and link		
22		PRO-002-002		Process	How to Create a Testimonial or Case Study Video		

As you can see, we prefix our files with whether they are a flowchart or systems document. Then we include the department category number, then the document number.

For example:

FLO-002-003 = This file is a flow chart. It sits in the Marketing department, and is the third core document in that department's folder.

Eventually you'll have a number of files within your department folders.

The next diagram shows what your files will look like after you've organized them this way. They'll all be numbered, hyperlinked into your Document Registry, and accessible with just a click.

Won't that be nice?

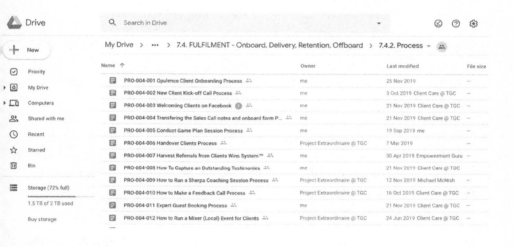

I've said it before and I'll say it again. <u>Information is everything.</u>

There are two areas of information your business must control: external and internal.

External information is your marketing - the image you're projecting to the world. Internal information is your operations - all the important files that help you run your business.

There's so many extra problems and wastage that occurs in business due to sloppy communication systems.

At The Game Changers, I had a lot of issues earlier on when I started to grow my team. Because it was very easy for staff to come along and create their own process documents, only to realize that they've already got three other processes documenting the same thing.

That's why nowadays every system document begins with the question: *Does a process already exist for this?* Then it's off to the Document Registry to check.

Information hijacking

Most companies have one or two people who have worked there for so many years, they're like a walking encyclopedia of your business. Got a question? Ask Cheryl. Not sure where something is? Ask Pete.

These people have been around your business, and have been involved in so many of its activities, that their knowledge is worth its weight in gold. Like an organic information hub, they can guide, advise, and otherwise help other staff members do their jobs easier and better.

The problem is that when they move on, they take all of that knowledge with them. For many business owners, this can turn into a kind of 'silent ransom' situation, where the owner is afraid of letting the employee go because they've been around for so long and know so much. Even if they're no longer right for the job.

Once again, this is an information flow problem. Your business needs information to flow freely internally for your staff to be able to do their jobs and help your business grow.

When information isn't organized according to this logical structure, it brings knowledge down to a per-person basis.

"Only Patricia knows where the new manufacturer's contact information is! And she's away for 2 weeks!"

"Glen was working on the January promo project, and he left without telling anyone where his project files were! I cannot find them!"

"Does anyone have access to D drive? I can't remember where Sandra saved her presentation!"

These information silos can cripple your productivity and lead to significant losses, in time, people, and money.

When your files are organized, staff can come and go without disrupting your business. Knowledge gets retained in your system, ready for the next person to pick up and use when employees move on.

Your wheels keep on turning, no matter who is pulling the cart.

Troubleshooting problems

There's a theory in Neuro-Linguistic Programming that goes like this:

Whatever you're achieving in life right now is a successful result of what you've done to get there.

If you're experiencing the same problem in business on repeat, it's because of the strategy you're running to create that situation...

The issue is not the result. The issue is the strategy that's being run again and again that's producing the result. And **the result is simply the logical conclusion of the steps within the preceding strategy.**

System or process failures in your business are the same.

Often I see business owners rolling out a new process, checking it maybe once or twice, and leaving it at that. I don't know about you, but I don't live in hope that things will work perfectly, because I know that they don't!

So at The Game Changers, when we roll out a new system, we also spend time on -

Applying and testing
Noticing where the shortfalls are

Filling the gap

Yes, this should be systemized too.

Here's a few ways to ensure your systems stay in a state of continuous improvement:

- Schedule a reminder every 6 months to review and update the process. Is there a better way to do it?

- Build a feedback loop into each system so that a staff member is checking that nothing (and nobody) is falling through the cracks.

- Assign a KPI to each part of the process, and make the person accountable for that part of the process *also* accountable for hitting that KPI every single time.

The fact is, 99% of tasks within your business are repeatable. But a lot of business owners think they don't have time to systemize them. So instead of spending 1 hour systemizing a 15-minute task, they'll spend hours repeating that 15-minute task over and over.

This is short-term thinking, and it won't get you very far. Using what you've learned in this chapter, you can begin to systemize your business quickly and easily.

It's time to go and map a process, and create a system around it (or get your staff to use the system for writing systems).

Download your systems template at: www.pathtofreedom.com.au/resources

Implement it. Use it. And then evaluate your results.

We'll cover the next stage of systems building in chapter 10, which is about automating your systems to run largely on autopilot.

Automation is the key factor that allowed me to scale my business to 7 figures with a small, remote working team. And it's what our The Opulence System™ members use to do the same.

You're going to love it!

AUTOMATION

AUTOMATION

"If you want to have more of an impact in business, you need to do less, not more. You need to focus on high-value activities - not just you, but your team too. Automating their repetitive tasks gives them more room to innovate and improve your business."

George Markoski - Positive Property Solutions

George is a vivacious, friendly guy.

He's the type of person other people gravitate to, although they might not know exactly why.

With an energetic presence and a bright friendly smile, the property game is perfect for George where, let's face it, presentation really matters.

George is an entrepreneur who started his property business from scratch at home. After creating a property portfolio that allowed him to 'retire' at age 37, George set his sights on teaching others how to gain freedom through property.

We caught up about a week prior to my writing this chapter. Naturally, our meeting was over Zoom - George lives about 2,500 kilometers away. And besides, we're under restrictions thanks to COVID-19.

George's friendly face fills my screen. He is pacing around his big, luxurious lounge room (he is trying out a new fitness gadget). Through the massive floor-to-ceiling windows fanning out behind him, I can see a 180-degree view of pristine Australian coastline and sparkling azure waters beyond.

Clearly, business is good.

But the road to George's success hasn't always been paved with granite. "When I started this business, a lot of the time I didn't know what I should be doing," he tells me. "So I got good at a lot of things. Now I realize that's not necessarily a strength... it can become a weakness. Because for me, I knew I could do everything, so I did. I just grabbed everything and did it myself. And that wasted a lot of time I could have spent on better things."

I ask George to stop pacing - he's making me dizzy. So he flops down on a plush oversized couch.

"As I grew my business, I took on staff," George continues. "But while that made things easier for me, it also made it harder in a way. Because now I was paying for their time. And the way my business was set up, a lot of that time was wasted. I had a lot of processes set up, but they involved repetitive manual work."

I smiled and nodded. "So what's changed from then to now, George?"

"Now I have a mantra that I try to embed in my staff," he says. "*If you do it more than once, find a way to automate it.*"

"That's a great mantra."

"I don't want my staff to waste their time doing tasks that can easily be taken care of by technology. I want them doing less work in general. Because when they're doing less task-based work, they can focus on innovation."

"Less work means more quality work, which is better for everyone," I agreed.

"Even if your team is doing 'quick tasks'.... that still eats up their day. Especially since every 15-minute job usually turns out to be a 45-minute job when you factor in interruptions, refocusing... it's all a waste of time and energy."

"These days I save myself - and my team - hours of unnecessary work every week by constantly pushing to delegate and automate," George continues. "Doing less task-based work also gives my team the space within their roles to deliver exceptional value to our clients. And that's good for everyone."

The conversation drifts off after that. We plan an impromptu holiday in Bali for a post-COVID-19 week of food, fun, and surfing.

Because we can.

George isn't trying to get off the call because he's got a million things to do. He's totally relaxed. He loves his business and enjoys working in it... but he's not enslaved by it. His systems are running. His team is focused on high-value activities that make his business better.

Like me, George can decide to take a week away at the drop of a hat, knowing his business will be run - and grow - without him.

Has George achieved total freedom in his business?

Not yet... but he's pretty close.

Do you remember those perpetual motion toys everybody had on their desks in the 80s?

If you're too young to remember, the most popular one featured a set of 5 metal balls strung in a row, suspended along a small metal stand.

When you pulled the end ball back and let it go, it would swing down and hit the next ball in the row. The energy from that strike would transfer from ball to ball, finally sending the ball on the other end of the row flying out. When it swung back in, it would hit the next ball in the sequence and start a new energy transfer in the other direction.

While not a true perpetual motion machine (perpetual motion violates the laws of thermodynamics, and we don't want that), it's pretty close. The kinetic energy transfer would keep the movement going for a long, long time.

Click, clack. Click, clack.

Or maybe you had the drinking bird toy when you were a kid. One pat on the head and that little guy would start bobbing, using the energy changes caused by the evaporating liquid inside it to swing its beak down, and up, down, and up.

Nothing happens in this world without *motion*.

Automation gives your systems a similar kind of effect.

Your systems tell your staff WHAT to do.
Automation prompts them to actually DO it.

It's the key to turning your systems from static documents (which can easily be forgotten) into *actions* that run on autopilot. Every day, week, and month. Or whenever you choose.

Because pretty much everything in business needs to be done more than once.

Invoices need to be sent. Emails need to be checked. Reports need to be compiled. And so on…

Automation keeps tasks going without anyone having to remember to do them.

Because we don't want to rely on any single team member to perform a role, right? We want our business to run independently. We want it to have no single point of failure.

So we build perpetual motion devices. As best as we can.

For your business, that's going to look like digital loops.

But before we begin, let me take you on a quick trip from then, to now.

My road to automation

Before I started The Game Changers, I built a business that required me to be there 24/7. I was stuck in the business in every way, especially physically (which I hated). After that business crashed and burned, I wanted to do things differently.

I had three things in mind for my new venture that would eventually become The Game Changers:

One: I wanted to make a huge impact and help a lot of people.

Two: I wanted to have a business that allowed me to work anywhere in the world.

Three: I wanted to be able to provide financial freedom for myself and for my family.

So, as I've advised you to do many times in this book, I started with the end in mind and reverse-engineered my way to my goal.

I researched. I studied. I learned everything I could to systemize my business so it could run without me.

Not because I wanted to *hit it and quit i*t. I love what I do and couldn't imagine ever stopping.

But until you have a business that runs without you, you have a job.

That was certainly what I learned in my first business. I had a multimillion-dollar job.

Every book I read taught me about writing how-to manuals and operating procedures. But in many ways, this material was outdated because it talked about creating a physical ops manual.

Physical manuals make sense for many businesses. You have your operational manuals sitting in the office, or on everybody's desk. When it hits a desk, it makes a satisfying thump. *Yep, lots of knowledge in there...*

This is how McDonald's operates. Maybe it's how your business works too.

But we've moved into a new era of business.

Millions of people work remotely across the world. At the time of writing this book, more people than ever are currently working from home due to Coronavirus-related restrictions on work and travel.

After things are back to 'the new normal' (whatever that may be), many companies will choose to keep their 'work from home' model, or at least some parts of it. Because it makes sense from a *lean* perspective.

Before this current crisis, 1000s of businesses were embracing lean principles. Many six and seven-figure businesses (including my own) operate with no big flashy office, and little overheads such as a large workforce and the bills that come with it.

Thanks to technology, the world is open. People from all countries can work together using the Internet to connect and share.

That's great for everyone starting a business now.

But back to 10-15 years ago, I couldn't find any information that addressed how to take my operations 100% online.

I started to create SOPs (standard operating procedures) anyway. It was a start, right? Soon enough I realized my team and I could just store them on Google Drive, and put them in their relative folders, and create an index of our files.

This file index is the document registry we spoke about in the last chapter.

Online file storage was a game-changer for us. Because I didn't have the time (or desire) to audit what they were doing all day, every day. Especially when I started to build an outsourced team, who were working on the other side of the world while I was asleep!

Reading through timesheets, following up about every little thing... to me, that's very archaic in the business world. And it's tear-inducingly boring. Although many businesses operated that way back then (and still do now), I believed that a greater currency was starting to emerge...

A currency around collaboration and contribution, and making a difference.

I knew that with the right culture in place, my team would be energized to perform their role. Not just for the paycheck, but because they felt a sense of fulfillment. Because they felt a sense of contribution. Because they felt a sense of being part of something far bigger than themselves.

I *knew* I could create the willpower in my team to work.

The other side of the coin was showing them what to do, and when... without the whole thing becoming a great big mess.

How could I make all my systems function seamlessly in a perpetually moving, automated way that kept us making progress towards our goals?

To figure this out, I needed to dive into behavioral psychology...

Habits and decision fatigue

Human beings are habitual creatures. We like to create habits and follow them, either consciously or unconsciously.

What's your routine for getting ready for work every morning?

What's your routine for going to bed?

What's your routine for meeting friends, for driving the kids around, or going to the gym?

You do things in a specific order. You perform a series of tasks to achieve an outcome (like walking into work with your clothes on).

What happens when something messes up your routine?

You get halfway to work and realize you forgot to put your watch on. Or you're not sure if you turned the hair straightener off. Or you forgot your piece of fruit.

Without routine, we kind of fall apart.

Because all of a sudden there's 500 micro-decisions to make every hour. And we only have a limited amount of brain capacity each day.

Mark Zuckerberg wears the same T-shirt every day, so he can save his 'brain power' for making more important decisions.

Albert Einstein famously didn't memorize his phone number, claiming that he didn't want to clutter his mind. He said, *"Never remember anything you can easily look up."*

Decision fatigue is real.

The more we can automate, the more brain capacity we save for bigger, more important work.

Knowing this, I started to think about how I could help my staff create routines for themselves. Even though many of them worked different hours, or only a couple of days a week, or on the other side of the globe.

How could I help them create a rhythm for each role?

As with most modern advancements, technology led the way.

One platform to rule them all

By 2017 we had systems for everything -

Running meetings
Onboarding clients
Managing finances
Training new staff
Creating systems
Managing time effectively
Rolling out marketing initiatives
Running client sessions

The thing was, many of these systems all needed different technology to run.

Active Campaign for emails and lead management.
Xero for accounting.
Slack for instant messaging among our team.
Hubspot for marketing and sales management.
Stripe for taking payments.

Every new piece of technology added another layer of complexity. Making it harder for my team to have absolute clarity on how to perform their role.

An online tool called Asana was the missing piece of the puzzle in allowing our business to truly scale and thrive independently of who was working in it.

There are many other tools that offer a similar result, but Asana is what has worked best for us. It's what we recommend our clients use too.

Asana helps us automate tasks, projects.. absolutely everything we do.

Nobody forgets to do a task within their role.
Nobody loses or misplaces information.
Nobody stuffs things up because they didn't know what to do.

And most importantly, if a staff member is away, we can give another staff member their Asana login, and they have access to everything they need to get the job done:

What to do

When to do it

How to do it step-by-step
The desired outcome (with examples)

Each task is hyperlinked to the system, flowchart, how-to docs, and anything else required. So by simply clicking on a task, anyone can literally follow along step by step. Even if they have never done it before.

Are they going to be as fast as your regular staff member? Absolutely not.

But will they get the job done to at least a 90% standard? Most likely.

And that's good enough until Cheryl comes back from her honeymoon, or until Greg gets over his bout of the flu.

The business operates no differently than the day before, even though there's someone else sitting in the seat. There's no disruption to clients or the rest of the team.

By automating your systems using Asana, your business will become so much more efficient that you'll probably find you don't need as many staff. Which means you can move your current staff to other roles in your Organisational or Accountability Chart, or exit them from the business and save some money.

Speaking of saving money…

Busting the '2-week training' myth

It's become almost normal for new employees to undergo 2 weeks of training before being expected to start delivering results in their role. The first 2 weeks are for watching over other people's shoulders, learning on the job, and basically having training wheels on.

That's a waste of everyone's time - and your money.

Every day your staff takes to get up-to-speed slows your business down. It affects your profitability, your clients... every department takes a hit now the herd is moving slower for the new calf.

Automating your systems gets your staff up-to-speed within *hours* on their first day.

So your managers don't have to micromanage - each role's task frequency is there in Asana. All new members have to do is follow the plan, and they'll succeed.

The combination of systems + automation is so powerful that when a team member moves on from The Game Changers, within two weeks of them giving notice we have a new staff member in and trained up in the role to take it over. Most importantly, the business doesn't miss a beat.

Before we implemented this, it would take us three months to get a salesperson on board and making sales. By using our systems + automation combo, we can have a salesperson making sales in their first week with us.

For admin-based roles, it happens even faster.

Setting up your first automation

Throughout this book, I've talked about the importance of having a clear file naming and organization structure. It's why you've been labeling files according to your business' departments.

The same structure that applies in your document registry and file structure also applies in Asana.

To quickly recap the process up until now -

Create a system, implement it, look at your results, and refine it until there are no further adjustments needed for it to give you the outcome you want.

Once there are no more adjustments to be made, it gets sent to the appropriate department head for their approval.

They may see some oversight that needs to be changed or adjusted. If not, they will name it correctly, file it within your internal structure, and add it to the document registry.

Here's where the automation part starts -

1. Add the system to Asana within the appropriate department.

2. Assign a team member to the new task or workflow.

3. Set it as a recurring task, in whatever frequency required.

4. Add the task description with the links to everything that's needed to understand and perform the task.

For example, just say the new task is your profit first allocation. That gets assigned to your finance admin and set up for actioning once a month.

Or the new task might be sending out a card on a client's birthday. That gets assigned to your customer service admin and set up for action once a year.

Naturally, we have a system for doing this which includes a template to ensure consistency.

Here's what a task looks like in our business:

You can see that the Asana task communicates who, why, when, what, and

---

[✓ Mark Complete]   📎 ⇲ 🔗 👍 … →|

Facebook Engagement posts *Inner Circle

Assignee	🌐 Salve Oc___No ⓐ
Due date	📅 Today
Projects	▢ 4a. Fulfillment Reoccurring Daily Tasks ⌄
Description	**Description:** This is the process that ensures that Weekly Facebook Engagement Posts (MWFSun) are posted, tracked and completed within scheduled time.

Process: https://drive.google.com/open?id='▨▨▨▨▨ , ▨▨▨▨▨

Templates: https://docs.google.com/document/d,"_"▨▨▨▨▨▨;7zQPa03U86ATVkxU/edit

Video Training:
https://www.useloom.com/share/7d▨▨▨ ▨▨▨▨▨▨▨▨

Subtasks

⊘ Post Monday

⊘ Post Wednesday

⊘ Post Friday

⊘ Post Sunday

---

how. It sits within a project, which sits within its department. It has process documents, templates, and video training hyperlinked within the task's description. And it has subtasks listed for each day the task is to occur each week.

For a staff member beginning their day, they log into Asana and see their task list, which compiles all of their daily, weekly, and monthly tasks in a list format.

Instead of performing their role ad-hoc (and potentially forgetting tasks), their entire day is laid out for them, every day.

What, how, and when.

It's kind of like 'paint by numbers' business.

And as I said earlier, people are creatures of habit. If they have to check 5 different platforms every day to do their job, they're just not going to do that.

Having ONE system for them to check every day makes setting up a routine super easy. They log in, look at their tasks, and get on with their day.

Sure we still use other platforms to get stuff done. We use Slack, Zoom, Zapier, and Active Campaign just to name a few. But the central hub is Asana, and we link out to those other platforms only when required as part of a task.

Using Asana means everyone in your business is running off the same system. At The Game Changers, we run our meetings, our processes, our projects, and our trainings out of Asana.

But you don't need to create the same degree of complexity yet.

Just get started with a couple of system automations and build out from there, remembering to keep your information structure intact.

Obviously, I cannot show you a demonstration of using Asana in this book.

This is why we've created a video to help you get started with Asana including a demo of how to set up your departments, projects, and tasks.

Find it at this link: www.pathtofreedom.com.au/resources.

Creating workers, not robots

All of this tightly controlled automation and systemization might be giving off a faceless vibe.

The goal here isn't to turn your workers into mindless drones.

But the fact is 99% of the stuff done in your business will need to be done again. And again.

So creating automated systems around these habitual tasks actually frees up your staff to be MORE creative and innovative. Because they don't have to think about every little thing each day.

Remember how earlier I talked about decision fatigue?

Studies show that we're only capable of really focused work for about 4 hours a day. So the more you can 'reduce the load' on your staff's brains by automating their roles, the more capacity they have for finding ways to be creative and looking for opportunities to make things better.

If you're worried that automating your systems will make your workers switch off, here's the antidote: CULTURE.

Your values and business culture even out the scale. They humanize your business and your people. Tasks are just tasks. The energy, creativity, and enthusiasm your team brings to their roles are what truly make your business shine.

We're not diving deep into culture in this book, because this book is about systemizing your business. If you're interested in building a strong A-player culture within your organization, get in touch with The Game Changers at www.pathtofreedom.com.au/go

Building feedback loops into your automations

Remember the Tesla autopilot mishap story from the last chapter?

The driver switched to Autopilot, totally ignored the road, and crashed.

Well, just like your KPIs, systems, goals, and everything else in your business, just because you've set this stuff up doesn't mean you can totally take your eyes off the road.

As with everything else we've covered so far, it's important to build feedback loops into your automations to ensure that nothing falls through the cracks.

A few things to include -

1. Once a new automation is set up, let the team member know where it is, what it is, and that it's been assigned to their name. Ask for a confirmation that they're good to go.

2. Asana gives managers the ability to pull all of the tasks that are overdue and check on them just with a click. So build in regular checks within each department head's routine that ensure their team members are completing their tasks and checking them off.

3. Create an automation that schedules periodic review of all automations within each department. The frequency of this is up to you - just don't 'set and forget'!

The key is to make sure that your automation system is kept up-to-date. Otherwise, nobody will know what the hell is going on. Your managers won't be able to monitor their staff's task completion. If someone is away, the person filling their role will be faced with a confusing task list that's messier than a dog's breakfast.

Disorganization brings your business back to a 1:1 level, where staff need to manually check in with each other, train each other, and follow stuff up via email (yawn). Congratulations, you've ended up back where you began!

Dealing with screw-ups along the way

In business (and life), problems are inevitable. You could even say that business is simply a series of problems to solve, in ascending order towards your goals.

Look, mistakes do happen. Even in a system that's near-perfect (perfection doesn't exist). But if the same mistake happens more than once, that's a problem.

Speaking for myself and my team, we love and welcome problems. Because problems let us know where there's a gap in our systems.

<u>Problems show us an opportunity to make things better.</u>
And that's a good thing!

But most business owners don't like problems, because it's something else to fix. So they ignore them, or apply a Band-Aid solution. And the same screw-ups keep happening and happening, taking up precious time and energy to fix.

If you've been problem-avoidant so far in your business, it's time to change your mindset. Rather than ignoring problems, or seeing them as a massive pain in the backside, you need to start looking for them.

Seek them out! You want to solve as many of them as possible. Not just when rolling out your systems and processes, but in business in general.

If that sounds too exhausting for you, here's what you need to do:

1. Get some coaching on your mindset. Because the bigger your business gets, the more problems you're going to have to solve. Connect with a Game Changers coach at

www.pathtofreedom.com.au/go

2. Let your systems do the heavy lifting. Every time there's a problem, the conversation needs to be:

Have we got a system for that?

Was the system followed?

If so, what did we miss?

If not, what happened and why?

Systems take the emotion and drama out of problem-solving.

Just say a client writes to you pissed off because a payment was taken out of his account despite him being switched to a payment plan.

Looking at your system, you could trace the problem back.

Let's say the cause was that someone hasn't updated their Stripe payment.

Was it a momentary lapse in concentration?

If so, is the staff member bored in their role? Is the best role for them within your business? Do they have other things going on personally that they need support with?

Or was it a problem with our system? Is there a gap or ambiguity in the process?

Either way, it's a problem that we welcome the opportunity to solve.

And yes, you should create a system for dealing with unhappy customers too.

Automating your first system using Asana

It's time to put this information into action.

Pick a system (or choose the one you wrote after the last chapter).

Jump into Asana and turn it into your first series of tasks.

As I mentioned before, I cannot show you a walkthrough of Asana in this book.

Which is why we've created a video to help you get started with Asana - including a demo of how to set up your departments, projects, and tasks.

Find it at this link: www.pathtofreedom.com.au/resources

HIRING

HIRING

"Set the bar high with who you're looking for, and follow up by giving your new hires the experience you promised: working for a company that is invested in them. Otherwise you'll turn A-players into people who don't give a damn."

Angus Thurston - Timberworx Unlimited

Angus treated hiring staff a bit like fishing.

He'd hire a bunch of people that had the basic carpentry skill required for the job, train them for three months, and 'throw back' the ones that turned out to be unsuitable. It was a constant cycle, rinse and repeat.

When he told me about this old strategy, I couldn't help but laugh.

"It's kind of the definition of insanity," I told him. "Getting to that three-month mark, realizing your time and effort has been wasted, and then thinking 'I'm just going to run that same pattern and hope I get a different result next time.'"

"Yeah totally," Angus agreed.

"But it's understandable," I add. "You're coming from a trades background, you hadn't been taught how to stuff like building a team. And you were so busy trying to run your business that you just kept pushing forward the only way you knew how."

When Angus started his journey in The Opulence System™, he was hurting.

His furniture business was growing, but he was spinning his wheels trying to find the right people. He was constantly putting out spot fires. His staff turnover was really high. His clients weren't getting what was promised. And it was costing him a small fortune hiring people, training them, firing them, and then going back to the drawing board again.

"The thing is, I saw evidence everywhere that good tradespeople were out there," Angus said. "I saw my competitors hiring good people and not working in the day-to-day of their business. But I just didn't know why I could not do the same. It was so frustrating."

I was familiar with that way of thinking. I'd heard it a million times.

Lots of business owners complain there are no good hires out there, but the truth is they just either a) don't have their business set up to attract A-players or, b) aren't communicating the value of working there clearly enough.

"So what's different now?" I was curious.

"I spent some time getting clear on who I wanted to employ. Just like I do with my marketing avatar, I defined what type of people they were, their values, their family life, and so on. I stopped thinking about the skills I needed, and started thinking about the whole person. And I built that information into my recruitment process."

"And that strategy is getting you different results," I stated. It wasn't a question - I'd seen his celebratory updates in our members' group.

"It's like night and day," Angus stated. "We put up an ad for an apprentice last month, and the first guy who applied was perfect for the job."

"So there *were* good staff out there... you just were attracting the wrong fish," I mused.

Angus laughed. "Totally. Now I know I can hire the right people for the right seats so to speak, it's given me much more confidence that I can grow and scale my business."

One of the hardest shifts you'll make is going from someone that works *in* the

business, to becoming someone that leads the business.Most small businesses start with the owner being the 'technician'. For those unfamiliar with Michael E Gerber's *The E-Myth*, the technician is the one 'on the tools', so to speak.

The designer. The plumber. The writer. The baker. The coach. A technician gets into business to make a living doing the thing they love.

They are passionate about producing a really good product or service. They put everything into it. Soon, word gets around. They find themselves with loads of work on.

But eventually they hit a plateau. There's just not enough time in the day to get everything done. So what to do?

At this point, most people hire some staff and, frankly, make a mess of it. (At least the first few times.)

If you've been struggling to attract good staff, or if your business feels more like a creche full of overstimulated toddlers than a cohesive group of A-players, what you're about to read is really important.

In the next couple of chapters, you're going to learn how to hire and retain great staff. People who run your business for you, almost as passionately as you. So you can fulfill your ultimate vision and live the lifestyle you want.

Once you learn how to attract, train and retain A-player staff, your entire business will change.

So will your life.

But before we dive into how to hire your next A-player, let's address a couple of mindset issues that, left unresolved, will hinder your best efforts.

Hiring blocker #1: It's your business, it's your baby

A study published in the March 2017 edition of the journal Human Brain Mapping found that entrepreneurs' emotional and brain responses toward their businesses resemble those that parents have toward their children.

To make this discovery, some very smart people gathered a group of business owners, wired their brains, and showed them a series of random pictures.

When the subjects saw a picture of their kids - *ding, ding, ding, ding!* The parts of their brain associated with emotional processing lit up like lighters at a Bon Jovi concert.

That's pretty much expected.

But when the entrepreneurs were shown pictures associated with their business... *the same thing happened.* Ding, ding, ding, ding! 'Blaze of Glory' must be on...

The study brings new meaning to the idea that a business really is an entrepreneur's baby.

In a sense, you've given birth to your business. You've raised it from a bawling toddler, guided it through its first steps, and watched it grow.

Leaving its care in the hands of someone else can be scary. Like Robert DeNiro eyeing off Ben Stiller who marries his daughter in Meet the Parents, you may feel like your new hire is never going to be good enough.

But here's the problem.

What we choose to believe influences how we experience our reality.
Let's look at three common limiting beliefs business owners have towards hiring staff.

1. I can't find someone that's reliable

2. I can't find anyone that's trustworthy

3. I can't find anyone who wants to work hard

When we choose these beliefs - either consciously or unconsciously - we start to energetically project that belief onto situations we experience. Our brain filters incoming data to highlight our 'goal' - proof that we were right.

Reality is subjective - what we believe, we see.

So if you hire a staff member while secretly believing they're all untrustworthy... chances are you'll unconsciously attract someone who *is* untrustworthy to prove yourself right.

The first step for resolving this is to accept that things will go wrong in your business. And to be OK with it. Not happy about it, of course. But OK.

Because then you can stop experiencing an emotional gut-punch every time something goes wrong, and focus instead on rectifying the situation and ensuring it doesn't happen again.

As counterintuitive as it may seem, the less emotionally entangled you are in your business, the better you can run it.

Remaining emotionally attached to every single outcome will wreak havoc on your heart and stop you from letting your business grow. Instead of seeking problems to solve, you'll be so afraid of making a mistake that you won't take steps forward.

At this point in this book, you've learned how to build systems the run different aspects of your business.

You've set up KPIs to track your progress and monitor your business' vital signs.

You've put feedback loops in your systems so that mistakes get rectified and processes get improved.

It's time to trust the structures you've put in place.

Shortly I'll show you how to attract people who are a values-match to your company. So you can trust your people, too.

For every parent, there comes a time when you've gotta let your child make their way through the world autonomously. Know when to let go of the training wheels.

On to number two…

Hiring blocker #2: Letting go of control

Most entrepreneurs are control freaks.

I say this with love. I'm a recovering control freak myself.

Of the thousands of business owners I've worked with over the last 10 years, the majority of them don't really want to let go of their 'role' in the business. Even though they're overworked and over it - deep down they don't want someone else coming in and taking over.

So instead of hiring staff and being willing to become the leader they need, the business owner holds on tight to every little thing. Or they sabotage their new hires because they simply don't trust anyone else to be as good at the job as they are.

"Only I can do it right."

"Nobody is as good at the job as me"

"Everybody else stuffs it up"

If you're feeling a pang of recognition here, that's ok. You're in a safe place.

But the truth is, there are hundreds of things that others can do just as well as you can. Or even better.

But you need to let go of your vice-like grip.

As you systemize your business on your journey to becoming its visionary, there will be many roles you're happy to hand over to a new staff member. But there will be one or two that you will find it hard to let go of.

For me, my perfectionist Achilles' heel was sales. I had no qualms against hiring people to do things I didn't enjoy doing, like bookkeeping, appointment scheduling, and so on. But for a long time, I couldn't let go of my belief that nobody could close sales for my business like I could.

I was the sales guy. I was the only one with the knowledge and understanding of my business to close new clients. Or so I chose to believe...

So I built my whole business around me doing all the sales calls. As you can imagine, it limited my business growth. Nearly burned me out, too.

But when I systemized my sales call process, so it was teachable to someone else... that opened a whole new world for me.

I could hire a sales team. I could train them on my system, and mentor them until they were as good as me (or better).

The same thing happened with hiring new coaches to provide support for our The Opulence System™ members.

Could anyone else coach like I could?

No, but there's talent out there that's just as exceptional, just in a different way. And these days I proudly have a group of coaches in The Game Changers' family who are absolutely outstanding and give the same amount of enormous value that I do if not even more.

The best part? Every other A-player I have in the team brings a different flavor. A different perspective. Different experiences and ideas.

The differences in my team bring new levels of richness to The Opulence System™ members. And that makes the business stronger. Instead of having one business coach to gain knowledge from (me), members have access to a group of coaches who all have different knowledge and experience to learn from.

If I had kept hanging on, clinging to the belief that only I could do the things I was good at... it scares me to think about how much my business would have been limited by my own inner control freak.

I'd probably be sitting in a messy office right now, clocking up 80+ hours a week, having a team that caused more problems than solutions, and blaming my lack of success on everyone else!

I know how hard letting go of control can be. To trust that other talented people can step into your shoes (and fill them).

But if you've hired the right people, and given them the resources they need to be successful in their role, it's time to get the hell out of the way. Let them bring their skill and personality to the business.

As long as your KPIs are on track to keep you moving towards your ultimate vision, outcomes are achieved, and everyone's living by your business' values, it doesn't matter if tasks are completed your way or theirs.

Hiring blocker #3: Your identity within the business

Because you've birthed this business and raised it from a young age, a lot of your identity is entwined within it. You're proud of what you're achieving. It gives you a sense of purpose. A sense of being needed. A sense of importance. You *matter*.

So when someone comes along to take some of your responsibility away... it can trigger your brain into sabotage mode.

As I've mentioned earlier in this book, our brains like to recreate experiences for us that are 'survivable'. You can survive working across 7 roles in your business (even if only for a short while).

So when someone comes along to take one of those roles away, you'll probably self-sabotage to protect your identity as 'the hard worker', or 'the underdog', or however you see yourself. Subconsciously, of course.

Because deep down, "I knew I couldn't find anyone as good as me," translates into: "I must be needed. I must be valued. I must be worthy."

It's why business owners keep working 80+ hours a week even when they've got a team around them. It's why whenever a workaholic lets go of the reins, chaos ensues and they have to step back in.

Whatever situation you're in now, on some level, there's an emotional payoff for being in it. If you're overworked and miserable, that payoff isn't a healthy one. But it's feeding a need in your psyche all the same.

You may think this is psychobabble rubbish. 'Of course I want to stop working so many hours Barry! I'm exhausted!'

Ok then... so why haven't you before now?

Is it because you can't find someone as good as you?

Is it because nobody is reliable? Or trustworthy? Or competent?

Maybe it's time to let go of a few limiting beliefs.

A belief isn't a fact. A belief is a conclusion we once decided to be true, and have stopped questioning.

Take 5 minutes to do a little mindset shifting with me right now.

If you believe you can't find good employees, ask yourself this series of questions. If your limiting belief is something else, just swap the words for whatever is going on for you. Sit and think about your answers for a few minutes.

1. Do I know of any other businesses that have good employees?

2. Are there other businesses like mine that have good employees?

3. If it's possible for them to find good staff, surely it's possible for me to find them too?

4. What belief do I have to change to attract good employees like others do?

Back in my earlier kitchen renovation business, I used to program all the custom jobs into the cutting machine. I *hated* it. I knew that owners of my competition weren't sitting at the cutting machine punching in dimensions all day. I knew they had people to do that job for them.

But even knowing this, I still couldn't attract someone who could do it for ME.

Looking back now, I know that being the only one who could program this monstrous machine gave me a sense of control and ownership of my business. Deep down, I didn't want to let go of that control. Because without that important job, who was I?

Think about one chore that you hate doing in your business. Something that's a $100 an hour task (you should be focused on $10,000 an hour tasks).

If you dig deep into your feelings about this task, what does your heart tell you? Do you get an emotional payoff from being the one who has to do it?

If so, it's time to let go, if not, time to look deeper… There's always a secondary gain. If nothing was stopping us having what we wanted we would already have it. Don't look too far, what stops us is not 'out there' it's 'in here' inside of your preprogrammed from your past life experiences.

How to hire A-player staff

At The Game Changers, hiring someone who fits the values is more important to us than hiring the perfect skillset fit. That approach has served us incredibly well.

The Opulence System™ members hire this way too, which is why they're able to exit the operations of their business within 6-12 months of joining the program when they apply what we teach.

A lot of business owners hire based on skill at the sacrifice of values. They want someone they know can do the job.

"Right now I just need a worker who can install cabinets. I'll figure out the rest later."

This is a mistake. And it often stops businesses from scaling. Because things have to change in order to scale. Businesses without a values buy-in from their staff get a lot of resistance when new initiatives are rolled out. They encounter more performance problems with their staff too.

The thing is, you can train someone to a certain skill level. Adam can be trained in cabinet installation and be up-to-scratch in a couple of weeks.

But you can't train someone to have a different set of values. At least, not easily or quickly. People build their values over decades, layering on more and more levels of belief through the experiences they have, and what they interpret those experiences to mean.

It's much easier to hire a values match from the outset than try and undo 30 years of conditioning!

Now you've identified what's going on behind the limiting beliefs that may be holding you back, let's look at how to actually make things happen.

The hiring process

By now you've created your organizational chart, you've used The Task Audit™ to identify which role to hire for first (or next), and you've written your position description for that role. How do you actually find someone who fits the bill?

The job ad

It seems simple enough. Write a job ad. Put it on a job board. Collect resumes. Find your golden goose. So why then can it get so hard?

When I go fishing, I use a different type of bait and lure to catch the fish I want. Recruitment is kind of the same (without the hooks and guts).

But most people expect the right fish to be attracted to whatever you throw out. That's not how it works. Boring job ads will attract boring people.

Instead of using the same cookie-cutter approach as everybody else, write your job ad in a way that attracts your ideal candidate. Similarly to how you write your marketing materials to attract your perfect buyer. How can you present the offer in a way that excites the ideal person for that job?

If you're writing a job ad for a creative, big picture kind of role, don't stuff your ad full of detail and specifics. Because a creative person will not be attracted to that kind of ad.

On the flip side, if you're writing a job ad for somebody who needs to be highly detail-focused, write your ad with absolute specificity. Don't get fluffy or use lots of creative flair. Somebody with the characteristics you want for an analytical role will be put off by too many hearts and rainbows. Whereas your ideal customer service hire might love that kind of thing.

Similarly to how you research your ideal client, get clear of who you're writing the job ad for. What are their traits and characteristics? You might even use a personality profiling tool like DISC or Myers Briggs to help you. Then make sure you're using language and words that appeal to that type of person.

Don't get this confused with the job description itself - that information remains the same. But the way you language it, and the way you present the job ad, needs to match the personality you're trying to attract.

I remember one client from a couple of years ago - Justin Bourne from Blank Canvas. When we started working together, he was doing $35,000 a month but he was working until 3am. Obviously, this wasn't sustainable. Or enjoyable.

So he tried to hire someone to help with the workload.

One day he rang me up and said, "Barry, I've had these two job ads running for ages. But I can't hire someone, no one's applying. What am I doing wrong?"

After talking with Justin for a while, I identified the first thing that was stopping him.

Justin had some unconscious beliefs around the way he identified with his place in his business. Deep down he believed that no one could do things better than him.

So first we focused on shifting the way Justin identified himself within the business. Before we could even consider touching anything else, this belief had to change. Because Justin kept attracting people who would prove his unconscious bias right.

Once that was taken care of, I looked at his job ads.

One of the roles was for graphic design. But the job ad was written with so much detail, that it read like visual granola. Boring as hell.

I asked Justin, "Who are you speaking to here? How can you write about this role in a way that excites a creative person to apply?"

So Justin thought outside the box a little. He reworked the ad to be a bit more fun and enticing. He asked applicants to create a digital banner advertising themselves and use it in their application. Within a week he had applications flooding in, and within two weeks he'd hired someone who was a terrific fit for the company.

The right lure gets the right catch.

Advertising your job ad

To advertise for roles at The Game Changers, we use our network first. We'll advertise on LinkedIn, reach out to our personal networks through social media, and ask our marketing database too.

This usually bears fruit. But if not, then we use both paid traffic on Facebook, and a popular job board in Australia called www.seek.com.au.

If you don't have a large network (yet), here's what to do.

Before running your job ad on a large network such as Seek, create a Facebook 'we're hiring' campaign. People overlook Facebook ads for recruitment but it's actually very effective. And thanks to Facebook's incredibly detailed targeting, you can advertise only to the kind of people you want to attract.

Facebook ads work out faster, cheaper, and more effective than throwing the net wide on a job network and spending hours looking through 100s of completely unsuitable resumes.

I won't go into how to set up Facebook ads in this book, because the platform is always changing. Plus it's too involved for what I want to achieve for this chapter.

If you'd like help setting up your recruitment campaign with Facebook ads, just get in touch with a Game Changers coach at www.pathtofreedom.com.au/go.

Automating your communication with candidates

Your job ad is more than a summary of what the role is about. It is also the beginning of a dialogue between you and your candidates.

Guiding them through a set communication structure sets the rules for their interactions with you, and saves your team hours of wasted time answering unsolicited progress enquiries.

Naturally, you'll systemize this process so it runs with minimal manual input from your HR staff. Here's the process to follow.

1. In your advertisement, clearly outline the cut-off date for applications, and let candidates know when they will get an answer from you.

2. Set up a recruitment page through Wufoo Forms or Google Forms, so people can submit details you're asking for and attach their CV.

3. Use Zapier to connect your recruitment page to your email automation software (we use Active Campaign). Tag new applicant details with the department and job they're applying for, then add them to an automated 'thank you' email sequence.

4. In your 'thank you' email, acknowledge their application has been received, and that they won't hear back from you until one week after the application close date. That gives your team enough time to shortlist candidates for the next round.

5. On the application cutoff date, create your first candidate shortlist. Shortlist between 15 and 20 people.

6. Tag the unsuccessful candidates to trigger an automatic email saying 'we don't feel at this point in time you're a fit, however, we'd love to keep your details on file for any potential future roles that come up'. It's best not to burn your bridges - and having a pool of pre-selected suitable candidates makes hiring for the role easier next time.

7. Send an email to the shortlisted people inviting them to a phone interview. Use call booking software like Acuity

Scheduling or Youcanbook.me to make things super easy, so your recruitment team doesn't have to waste their time on the low-value task of appointment setting.

8. Conduct initial phone interviews. We've created a phone interview template for you. It lists all the questions we ask and has space for you to record answers and give a good, better, best rating for all applicants, so it's easier to sort through them later.

9. Score each candidate's answers from 1-5, and enter those scores into a spreadsheet.

10. Shortlist the top performers for 2nd round interviews. Tag the unsuccessful ones to trigger the same rejection email you sent to those who didn't make it in round 1.

11. Time for round 2 interviews. This interview goes a bit deeper. The questions asked here are designed to elicit responses around personal values. We've created a template for you to use with all the questions you'll need - download it at this link www.pathtofreedom.com.au/resources

12. Invite the top 3 candidates from round 2 into panel interviews. If you have an integrator or HR manager, they should take care of the process up until this point. If you're hiring for a senior role, then you can get involved in the panel interview if you choose. If you're hiring for a junior role, let your department heads and Integrator conduct the interview.

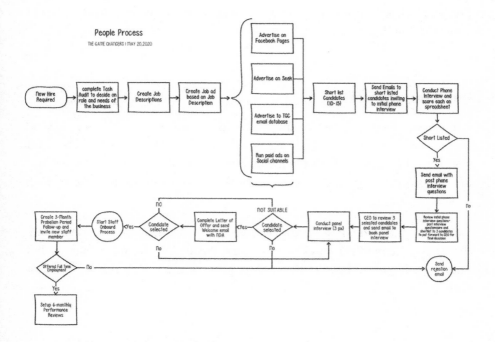

The panel interview

Include a few different people who are relevant to the role advertised. Earlier on, when I didn't have the support I now have around me, I had some of my current employees form that panel. That helped them feel part of building the team.

If I'm interviewing for a coaching role now, I have my coaches on that panel interview. If I'm interviewing for the sales role, I have my sales team on that panel interview. Because they know the role. Also they're going to be working closely together, so it's really important that they're the right fit for that department.

As for the interview itself, the structure is loose with no formality. It begins with everyone having a casual chat and building rapport. Then my team will ask some rapid-fire questions to see how the candidate performs under pressure. The goal here is to connect and get a gut feeling of how much value the candidate will bring to the team.

Offering the role

After you've selected the winning candidate with the panel's input, send them a letter of offer, a welcome email, and an NDA to sign. This is all systemized of course, with templated emails and workflows set up in your email automation platform (such as Active Campaign) and of course, Asana.

But don't reject the other candidates yet just in case, for whatever reason, the selected candidate chooses not to go ahead. Let the others know that you're reviewing things and you'll be back to them within a week. That way, if the candidate doesn't accept the role, you've got your backup ready to go.

If they do accept the role, tell the other candidates they weren't successful. Keep them in your candidate pool for other job options in the future - the more candidates you have already pre-screened and qualified, the easier hiring becomes.

Some roles may even emerge that a previously unsuccessful candidate would be a great fit for. That's how you can hire great people really quickly.

Upon role acceptance, your new hire starts the onboarding process with a three month probation period.

If all goes well, once they're fully on board, set up six-monthly performance reviews and annual remuneration reviews. This becomes a system that sits in your 'People' department within Asana.

Onboarding new team members

The most important part of the onboarding process is that new staff get taken through the vision, mission, and values of the company first. Then take them through the software systems they're going to be using in their role, including Asana, which has their daily, weekly, and monthly tasks ready to go.

The end goal is to set up the entire onboarding system within Asana, so it's literally 'click and learn'. A systemized onboarding process means a team member doesn't have to sit with new hires day in, day out to take them through their role. Instead, they go through a set series of introductory lessons at their own pace.

But it's not an inhuman process - schedule meetings with other team members into their onboarding journey too. Ensuring there are regular catch-ups and touchpoints with others in their team helps them assimilate into the company culture too.

If you haven't got any systems and processes set up and you're hiring from scratch, there's no better time to create your onboarding process. While you sit with your new hire and take them through everything, record it.

Record it on Loom, record it on Zoom, or record it via audio, and then have that team member build their journey into an automated onboarding system. So the next time you need to hire for that role, you've got everything ready.

As with everything in your business, your goal is to touch it only once. Then systemize and automate.

Firing staff

A chapter on hiring wouldn't be complete without talking about the flipside.

Sometimes despite the best of intentions, you'll get it wrong. Someone who seemed to be a great fit at first just doesn't work out. Or perhaps you decide that an old staff member isn't living your company values and has to go.

The cost of keeping somebody that isn't the right fit is far greater than the short term cost of having to reinvest time and energy into finding someone new.

For many business owners, firing staff is an upsetting experience. For both parties involved! At best, someone walks out with a sullen grudge. At worst, tears and tantrums.

I'll never forget the first employee I had to let go. Although I felt better once the Band-Aid had been ripped off, so to speak, my anxiety around having The Firing Conversation was gut-churning.

But looking back at every single staff member I've ever let go, firing them has always been 2 or 3 months overdue.

Because you know when someone's not working out. But you keep putting it off. You give them more resources to help them improve. You hope that things will change. But they don't. And you have to fire them anyway.

At the end of the day, delaying making the call to let someone go costs both you and them pain and wastes both of your time. I've had staff that have thanked me for making them redundant. Because they knew they weren't a fit, but they didn't have the guts to make the call. Or they were worried about letting the team down.

Equally too, I've had team members thanking me for making the decision to let someone go who wasn't living the company values.

It's your job to make the tough choices.

Think of your team as a second family of sorts. You must protect that family. You're the papa bear. Or the mama bear. They're your cubs. I'm not saying you should swipe the face off of anyone who wanders by, but you've got to make the hard decisions that benefit your tribe.

Your staff are looking at you as a leader. If you are allowing substandard behavior, you're actually unconsciously saying to all your other staff members that that's okay.

As a leader, you must be clear on what you expect, and who you want to take with you. If you're living congruent with your company values, the right people will show up. They will fight to protect their culture. And they will expect you to do so as well.

The firing conversation

Too often, this conversation feels like a breakup. There's so much emotion on both sides, and so much anxiety, that it becomes a total mess.

Instead of slamming the hammer down and trying to get your ex-employee out of the office without them breaking anything, there's a better approach.

Sit down and have a conversation about *them*. Ask if they're happy in their role. If they're enjoying the work. If they feel they are fitting in with the culture of your business.

In short - have a conversation with them from a place of love, not judgment.

By shifting the conversation from 'you're not performing' to 'how do you rate your own performance'... you shift the energy from finger-pointing to curiosity.

You're not having a go at them. You're asking them how they honestly feel they're doing in the role. When the conversation shifts from being accusatory to inclusive, it's very hard to get defensive.

And besides, employees know when they're not doing so great.

When you decide they're not footing the bill, they just feel it. Whether consciously or not. So by having open honest conversations about how they're *really* going, it opens the space for them to bow out gracefully and save face.

Which is much more preferable than the usual 'shock and awe' campaign where you tell them they're fired, and it hits them out of nowhere, and then they feel wronged, and then the battle-axes come out!

The bottom line is, if you're not willing to protect your team and your culture from negative influences - even ones from within - you shouldn't have a business. Because being in business means being responsible for the wellbeing of everyone. You can't do that if you allow someone to hang around that's not a values fit.

If there's someone in your organization that's bringing the team down, it's time to let them go. The rest of your team will thrive without them. And so will you.

It's time to systemize your hiring process. That means building a flow-chart of your process, creating tasks in Asana (or whatever management software you choose to use), and assigning the responsibilities and accountabilities to someone in your organization. If you're a solo operator, you'll assign them to yourself. Just for now.

As always, we've done the heavy lifting for you, so you can get started faster.

Download our flow chart of the hiring system and interview questions at this link: www.pathtofreedom.com.au/resources

YOUR TEAM

YOUR TEAM

"As the business owner, it's not my job to dictate and micromanage my team's every move. It's my job to facilitate the resources and environment they need to perform their role optimally, and then get out of their way."

Pete Maunder - No Limits Basketball

"What the hell am I doing this for?"

It's 2am on a Sunday morning, and Pete is sitting in his garage, his eyes straining under the dim light of a single bulb.

Piles of basketball jerseys surround him. Unopened boxes wait to be counted. Pete's fingers shake in the cold as he notes each jersey's size on his stocktake sheet. He puts down his pen. He swats away another moth.

"Why am I counting jerseys at 2am when I have five staff??"

Pete started off as a sole trader, building his basketball training business up from scratch. But as he started bringing on employees, he still thought of himself as a solo operator. He told his staff what to do, and how to do it.

For a long time, he wore his hard work as a badge of honor. He was hustling. He was grinding. Just like Gary Vee... right?

But not surprisingly, he was bone tired. And kind of pissed off at everything. Was he actually getting it a bit wrong? Was this really what being an entrepreneur was about?

In his recent The Opulence System™ Hot Seat interview, Pete looks back and laughs.

"A year ago, I did everything myself - even though I had a team," he explains. "I believed that my team wasn't as capable as I was, so I limited their function in my business. I didn't let them think on their own. I just had them follow the very detailed plan I put in place."

"This was nothing to do with them," he asserts. "It was my mindset - that was the problem. My perfectionism was eating me alive. I was so stuck in thinking things should be done exactly the way I would do them, that I limited my business growth. Pretty ironic for a business that's literally named 'No Limits Basketball'."

I understood what was going on. Pete's mindset hadn't quite switched over from *employee* to *leader*.

That is, until that morning when Pete found himself in his garage, counting jerseys at 2am. Why was he, the leader of the business, sitting in the cold and doing a task he could pay his 12-year-old niece five bucks to do?

That was his first 'aha' moment.

Eventually, Pete learned to let go of control and gave his team the freedom to do their jobs. Putting systems and processes in place helped ease his tight grip on every little detail.

Not surprisingly, Pete soon realized that his team could do many things much better than he could. Trust built between Pete and his team. His team gained a level of autonomy that allowed them to shine. And Pete started to step back and focus on the bigger picture.

In our Hot Seat conversation, I can't resist pointing out the obvious.

"You're a basketball coach, right? You teach kids to play as part of a team. But you weren't teaching your own staff to work as a team. But you were determined to operate as a Lone Ranger for so long. You were great at building teams on the court, but not so much in your own business."

"The irony never stops," Pete chuckles.

"Fast forward to now, and I let them do perform their roles as they see fit," he says. "I tell them the outcome I want to achieve, and let them work out the best way to get there. And they do a really good job of that."

Pete is starting to experience the freedom that a systemized business with a solid team gives. He can expand his business because his other trainers are just as good as him. He can go to training camps and be completely away from his business for a few days, knowing everything will run smoothly.

"The best part is that I can tell my team enjoy their roles a lot more," adds Pete. "They use words like 'we' and 'our' when they talk about the business. They have a feeling of ownership and personal buy-in about our vision, mission, and values. They don't just clock in and clock out anymore - they are invested in the outcomes we're collectively trying to create."

"You're not playing an individual sport anymore," I tell him. "You're all playing as a team."

"Yeah," Pete agrees. "And it's so much more fun than doing it alone."

Your business' ability to grow and thrive depends on the people you gather around you to perform the roles you don't have the time or experience for.

Your customer service staff. Your bookkeepers. Your sales reps. And so on. If they don't do their job well, your business falls apart.

Perhaps not surprisingly then, complaints about staff make up about 80% of the gripes I hear from business owners.

"My team are lazy"

"Everybody leaves in less than a year"

"If I'm not there, everything goes to hell"

"My staff don't care about quality like I do"

Years ago I read a quote that really stuck with me. It went something like this -

"Hire the best people and then get the f*ck out of the way."

That's well and good enough… but it's only half the equation. Because sure, you can give them your systems and an Asana login so they know how to do their job.

But even the best people need motivation. How do you make them 100% dedicated to the role? How do you make them want to stay at your company?

In a nutshell: *culture.*

Culture is the beating heart that drives your systemized business. It's that spark that makes your team want to show up. It makes them excited to work hard. It makes them productive, happy, and loyal employees.

A few years ago, I spoke about leadership at an SEO agency in Perth. The agency dominated its market because of its exceptional service and results.

Many of its employees had been there for 20 years. During those years, some of them had been headhunted by competitors.

I asked them, 'Why didn't you take the new gig?'

They answered - 'I love working here. They (management) do a lot for us. We have a great working culture. I don't want to risk leaving for more money and losing what I've got here. I'd rather stay, earn a little bit less, but enjoy my job more. Overall it's worth it.'

Running a team is not about hiring a bunch of people and taking your hands off the wheel. It's about actively building a tribe, a kind of second family. It's about creating a team that has got your back, and know you've got theirs, regardless of where the business is at.

Master business-builder Richard Branson put it best -

"Train people so well that they can leave, but treat them well enough so they don't want to".
In this chapter, you'll learn how to do just that.

Creating your company culture

By now I'm sure you've followed the earlier stages in the book, and you're clear on your vision, mission, and values. You've set your goals and worked out which roles you want to hire for first.

You've advertised a position description that attracts the right talent, and you have an interview process that weeds out those who aren't a fit.

What do you do with your new hires? How do you build a stronger team with your existing staff? Where does culture come into it?

Culture embodies the attitudes, morals, customs, and behavior shared by a group of people. Just like different cities and countries have their own culture, so does *your* group of people - your team.

Your culture stems from your *values*.

As we covered earlier in this book, your values define how everyone in the business shows up, every day. They're the living, breathing DNA of your business. They're not 'set and forget'. They need to be discussed, demonstrated, upheld, and defended when necessary.

Culture takes work. Neglect it, and it will rot. Feed it, and it will grow and thrive.

In a thriving business culture, your team will hold each other (and themselves) accountable to the business' collectively-held values. They'll have the hard conversation when a team member isn't meeting the standard. They'll talk about the values with each other, and actively seek to bring them into everything they do in their roles.

Why this is important now more than ever

Over my last 18 years of business, I've noticed a significant power shift between boss and employee. Gone are the days where people would get a job straight out of high school, stay with the company their entire working life, and then retire.

Now there are more employment opportunities than ever before. Statistics indicate that the average person will change jobs approximately 15 times in their life. Millennials are showing favor of job-hopping every few years to stave off boredom and refresh their skills.

And that's just the start of it. These days anyone can go online and start their own business. I'm writing this book during the COVID-19 crisis, where more people than ever are looking for ways to make a living without relying on an employer.

All this means that employers don't have the power they enjoyed in the past. Decades ago, the balance of control sat firmly with the boss. Businesses had hierarchical structures, kind of like the military.

If you didn't like something, you had one choice: fall in line or be fired.

When I started in business, that's how most organizations were set up. So my kitchen and bathroom renovation business evolved with a similar military-style power structure, simply because I knew no other way.

This was back before I began my business self-education, so my only point of reference was old bosses… and they certainly weren't great examples!

When I first went into business for myself, my only practical experience of motivating a team was, funnily enough, during my apprenticeship.

After showing great aptitude at the 'hands-on' part of my role, my boss decided it was the logical choice to have me lead a team of six other cabinet makers. Many of whom had been working for over 20 years.

I experienced a huge amount of push back. *Who is this young punk telling us what to do?* I wasn't respected, I was paid a quarter of their wage, yet somehow I ended up the one leading them. Even though I had no leadership ability.

This was a trial by fire… and I failed! What an incredibly valuable life lesson!

Coupled with the fact that I was a young guy with a lot of arrogance at the time, it didn't make for a very healthy mix. Nor did it provide me with the skills or the education I needed to be able to build a high-performing team.

These days, the team at The Game Changers are A-players who love their jobs and bring their best selves to work. But it was a difficult road to get here. That is, until I had some significant realizations about what people really want, and how I myself was showing up as a leader.

Building momentum and self-leadership

Through my earlier experiences of my poor leadership causing teams to rebel against me, I started to realize there must be a way to build a team that largely leads themselves.

Think of a rowing team. If you've got a team of 12 rowers all rowing in one direction, you've got momentum. If one person stops rowing, it creates a significant amount of drag. And it creates more work for everyone else on board.

The key is to create performance-based roles. You've done this when you created your Accountability Chart a few chapters ago. Performance-based roles combined with a strong culture means you don't have to check in on timesheets, or follow up staff to see if they were doing their job. That's a really limited way to run a team.

I realized that if I spent the time I'd previously spent on managing KPIs and timesheets on understanding our staff's core drivers, then we'd develop a self-perpetuating culture.

So I started to build a team that wanted to be actively involved in the hiring decisions of new staff. They wanted to actively be involved in sharing and letting us know when they felt a team member wasn't pulling their mark because as a whole, they felt it.

We've managed to build an organization where if a team member starts to drag their feet, others will step in and step up. Others will step in to educate, to help, to understand. To work with those team members to ensure that everyone's rowing at the same speed, at the same time, in the same direction.

Because everyone's bought into the vision, mission, and values. They're not posters on a wall, they're <u>commonly held beliefs</u>.

Your goal is for your team to drive their own momentum. And in order for them to have momentum, there's a couple of things that need to be in place.

1. **Clear outcomes.** A scoreboard is a great way to motivate a team. So use the KPI tracker you created in chapter 8. Teams can track their progress, and see the difference they're making with their projects and outcomes. Every team needs to feel that they're winning - in sport and in business.

2. **Accountability.** This isn't about your managers having to spend hours each day chasing things up. I'm talking

about self-accountability and peer-accountability. I'm talking about inspiring and supporting your team to self-regulate.

But it's not just up to them. The biggest accountability is on you as a business owner. It's your job to help them fill their bucket list, their dreams, their goals. Or they'll find a better place to work that does.

Here's where to start...

The real reason good staff leave

Think about your staff right now.

Do you know what their goals are?

What do they want from their lives?

How do they need to be recognized?

What is their love language or personality profile?
What motivates them to bring their best to work?

The answers to these questions are what truly makes your team run. Not time cards or meetings.

As humans, we're pre-programmed to want to be green and growing. Every living thing is pre-programmed to grow. If we're not growing, we're simply dying. No-one wants to feel that way. Yet so many employees are feeling stagnated and rotting.

Because they're not having their core needs met.

Most people spend the majority of their lives at work. Eight, nine, or even ten-hour days, 5 days a week, 50 weeks a year.

People don't switch off their humanity during this time. They still need to receive certain things to feel like they're 'green and growing'.

Tony Robbins says that at every level, us as human beings, we have six core needs.

Four of these needs relate to our physical being:

> One: the need for certainty and stability.

> Two: the need for variety and adventure.

> Three: the need for significance. To feel important.

> Four: the need for love and connection.

The last two relate to our spiritual being:

> Five: the need for contribution, to contribute to something bigger than ourselves.

> Six: personal growth. To be 'green and growing'.

We need these needs fulfilled at work just as much as at home.

And the more you can meet those needs for your team, the more loyalty, dedication, and passion they will bring to your business.

Sure, money is great. And sure, you can relate it to our core needs in a secondary way. But it's not a primary driver. Even if we think it is.

Money might relate to growth. It might relate to contribution. It might relate to how significant we're feeling. It might also relate to the certainty we need to provide for our family.

But money is not a core need. It's a vehicle for facilitating a few of them. That's all.

Employees never leave because they want more money. That's the excuse they use, and that's how they justify and validate it to themselves. Because it makes sense. Money makes the world go round, right?

Some people will leave if they don't have certainty. Does their job have a future?

Or they might not feel significant. Are they ever recognized for the great work they do?

They might not feel a connection with their peers. Do your staff members build relationships with each other? Or are they virtually strangers?

Perhaps they're not experiencing personal growth. Their role does not challenge them anymore, and the company gives them no pathways to bigger challenges.

People whose core needs are not being fulfilled will wander away in search of greener pastures. It's not about the money - the true currency of work is <u>fulfillment</u>.

Creating a culture that meets your people's core needs

Certainty doesn't just come from a regular paycheck. It comes from providing certainty of job security to your employees. People need certainty that they're being looked after, that they're taken care of, that they're heard, that they're understood, and that there are growth opportunities available to them.

When it comes to variety, this relates to what I covered in the chapter 10 about systems automation not turning your team into a pack of robots! Don't keep them stuck in mundane 'task-based' work 100% of the time.

Your team need to have permission - and encouragement - to be creative. To innovate. To think outside the box. But in a systemized way so they don't just start making changes and breaking things.

It's also important to understand that each person's 'variety limit' is different.

Some team members need the certainty of doing the same thing, day in, day out. That's how they perform best - when they can slip into their flow with no big surprises. They actually don't perform very well if there's too much variety.

Whereas others *need* variety. They get bored easily in monotonous roles. They thrive in roles where they're faced with new challenges every day.

Roles where they need to be creative and solve problems and pivot. That excites them.

Thinking about a few other core needs -

Significance is a big one, and it's something that drives a lot of discontent. How often do you praise your staff when they do something really well? How much negativity do they cop from you? Do they feel their ideas are heard? Do they feel respected? Do they feel like they matter? Or do they get shut down in every meeting?

Let's consider love and connection. People want to feel that they're more than just sitting in a cubicle every day and punching a keyboard. There are plenty of ways to bring love and connection into your team -

Hold regular 'family lunch' where you shout them a meal and everyone eats together. Have 'Member of the week' awards where the team votes for someone who has been living the values highly that week. Have a little presentation, make a big deal out of them. This meets the winner's need for significance too.

You can organize regular activities where the team does something outside of work. Ten-pin bowling. An escape room challenge. Hire a fishing charter. Movie night.

A few of these and you'll soon notice your team is working more cohesively and enjoying their job more. Because the need to belong sits at the heart of who we are as human beings.

Historically, grouping together has protected us from death due to starvation, exposure, or wild animals. While these days there's no saber-toothed tiger crouching behind the photocopier, we still feel that need to be part of a 'pack'.

Last comes the need for contribution. People want to know they're making a difference.

This need is usually the need that emerges after other needs have been met. It's at the top of Maslow's 'Hierarchy of Needs', which align loosely with Tony Robbins' 6 Core Needs.

When a person's basic and psychological needs are met - they have certainty their job is safe, they have connection with their team and feel important in the group - that's when people start to look towards helping others.

Think about billionaires like Richard Branson who have achieved pretty much everything they can on a personal level, so now dedicate their lives to philanthropy.

The need for contribution can exist just in someone's particular role, or to their team, or to the greater community.

When my team join us, many have a desire to help humanity at a global level. So our vision - *To Activate Every Being's Truest Potential and Experience Life Beyond Their Wildest Dreams* - is a big factor in attracting them to apply for their role.

Your department heads - and your integrator - should be acutely aware of their team members' personality profile. And they should tailor their leadership style to fit each individual's needs.

Getting your members to do a DISC profile is a great way to understand their unique personality profile. When you understand what they value, and their core drivers, you then know how to motivate them and keep them happy in their role.

For example, employees with a high need for significance might need a 1:1 meeting each week where they can express their feelings and feel heard.

Members with a low drive for significance might not need that extra attention. But they might value personal growth highly, and need access to extra training and career progression to keep them fully engaged within the company.

I won't cover leadership in full here - it would fill another book. Perhaps I'll write a book on my lessons in leadership in the future. But for now, if you want assistance in leading your team in accordance with their individual needs profile, get in touch with a Game Changers coach at www.pathtofreedom.com.au/go

"Winning the week"

If you're operating a business of ten people and above, you need to be having a weekly team meeting at a minimum. And then, ideally, a department meeting with the head of each department.

We teach a structure for weekly meetings called 'Winning the Week'.

It sets a weekly rhythm to ensure that we celebrate wins, monitor core metrics that matter, review project milestones, and discuss any issues.

Here's how it goes -

Start with wins

Before jumping into 'talking business', we create a positive energetic vibe.

To do this, we each bring a 'win' to the conversation. Not only does this put everyone in a great mood and lift the energy, but it also helps train your team to *seek the good.*

Where focus goes, energy flows, and results show...

What are we proud of personally?

What has the team done great?

What are our clients happy about?

Starting with a win from everyone only takes a few minutes. Don't underestimate the power of focusing on the great things you're doing, and the great results you're achieving.

We've even rolled out the concept to our The Opulence System™ members. In our private Member's group, we share our wins regularly and celebrate together.

We find that the more we share, the more we have to share.

And the more we share, the more opportunity we have to connect, champion each other, and reconnect with the FUN in business. Because business should be fun!

KPI tracking

Next - we look at our Scorecard and go through our KPIs.

Every team member updates whether they're on track, or they're off track with their progress.

Then we do the same with each project. If they're on track, great. If they're off track, the team member responsible for the project can put their hand up and ask for help. Then we all discuss solutions and decide on actions to resolve any issues.

Announcements

This bit's pretty straightforward, yet still important.

What's coming up for the business this week?

Are there any new hires onboard?

Any significant world events?

Any staff on holiday? Who will be in charge of their responsibilities while they're away?

Illuminating bumps in the tracks ahead allows you to keep the business running smoothly, regardless of what's going on internally or externally.

Issues aka 'The Shit Bits'

What challenges need to be discussed as a team?

This is where everyone gets a chance to bring up whatever is bugging them. Could be about the business, another staff member, or something personal that's affecting their work.

This is done in an honest, open way. It's not an invitation to argue. The 'shit bits' is a safe place for an open and honest discussion about issues that are affecting the team.

Because those issues, left unresolved, will fester.

Encouraging your team to raise issues during the 'shit bits' part of the meeting means your team is always emptying their tank. Negative emotions and volatility don't build up. Things get held in the light, discussed, and resolved.

Stars

Every week each team member gives a 'star' to another team member who is living the values. What did they do, and what value does it relate to?

For example, Rhonda could observe Frank going above and beyond for a client who needed extra help. So Rhonda acknowledges Franks' demonstration of Value #5: Outstanding service.

Stars are a great way of lifting the positive energy back up after 'the shit bits'. They're a way to keep the company's values in sharp focus. And they're also a great bonding mechanism for the team.

To-dos

Accountability time. Here we list and record the commitments that team members agree to complete within the next 5 days to be reviewed at the next weekly meeting.

Those get turned into tasks, and systemized in Asana.

Score

The purpose of weekly meetings is to connect with each other, to resolve issues, and to keep projects moving forward. These are high-value activities. Meetings shouldn't be boring - they should be energetic, positive, and productive.

And it's up to everyone in your team to make them so.

So to wrap things up, have each team member score the value of the meeting from 1-10. Then ask them to provide feedback on how to improve that score next time.

Running our weekly meetings this way has skyrocketed the value of those meetings for The Game Changers. Our Opulence clients report exceptional improvements in their team's solidarity, commitment to completion, and the energy they bring to their role too.

To help you start 'winning the week', we've created a template you can use as a run sheet for your weekly meetings from now on.

Download it at this link: www.pathtofreedom.com.au/resources

Handling resistance from your team

Often when a business owner wants to start implementing new innovations, they experience a lot of resistance from the team.

It's like trying to push a balloon under water. You can push it down to some degree, but as soon as you release the pressure, that balloon is coming back up through the surface.

It's the same with your team. The more they feel their free will is being repressed, the more they will desire for it to be *expressed*.

This often happens particularly when the business has been running for a few years without any systems or culture, and then the business owner suddenly introduces them.

Staff may feel like this is another one of those 'great ideas' that never get seen through. Or they might not feel personally aligned with the new culture and values, and want to go back to the old way of doing things.

Or, they feel this just something else 'management' wants them to do. *"We're already busy. Now we have to do this too?"*

Then everything that's unresolved within your team bubbles to the surface.

People rebel against the pressure. Some resign. Others develop a bad attitude.

I remember early on with The Game Changers, I had a lot of resistance from my team because things were constantly changing. Most people are programmed with a high drive for certainty. Lots of change wears them down.

And when you're building a business, especially those first years, not everything is going to work. So things will need to keep changing rapidly as you find your feet.

If your team is hugely resistant to change, that's going to slow you down.

If this is your experience right now, the most effective way to bring your team on board is <u>communication</u>.

Share with your team that, yes, you're in a growth phase of business, and yes, things are going to keep changing. And they're going to keep changing until the business reaches stability.

There's an opportunity here to show vulnerability in your leadership. I'm a strong believer in the power of vulnerability. The more your team feel a connection with you as a human being (not some distant boss), the easier it is to work with them.

So talk to them like a human being. Let them know that while it might seem like there's more work at the beginning, the reason you're making these changes is to make their jobs easier and more fulfilling in the long run. So, short term pain, long term gain.

When your team starts seeing and feeling the benefits of your changes, that's when you'll get more buy-in from them.

It's kind of like a plane taking off. Often the bumpiest part of the plane ride is the take-off and the landing, because that's when you break through turbulence. But when you get to altitude, it's often smooth sailing.

Dealing with guilt as you step back

Six weeks before writing this chapter, I was sitting in Bali and chatting to a friend. She asked me: "Don't you feel guilty that you're in away drinking from a coconut and surfing while your team is working?"

"Absolutely not."

Yet, it wasn't always like that. I remember in the beginning, I felt terribly guilty if I wasn't the first one in and the last one out. Just like Pete, I thought that showing leadership was proving that I was the hardest-working member of the team. I thought that this was 'leading by example'. But it's not.

Leading by example is actually living in accordance with the VALUES of your business. It's not working 80 hours a week because you want to be 'one of the team'.

You're not 'one of the team'.

You're not the accounts admin. You're not the VA. You're not the sales manager.

You're the visionary. The leader. The director of the business' future. And of the future of everyone within your organization.

They're depending on you for their livelihood. They're depending on you to feed their family. To pay their medical bills. To pay their rent or mortgage.

Even more so, they're depending on you for giving their time at work some *meaning*.

We spend the majority of our time at work. Your staff are giving up time in their life that they'll never get back... so it's your duty to make sure that their needs are met during that time.

It's your job to make sure that they have a sense of connection. Purpose. Enjoyment. Appreciation. Recognition. Those are the core human drivers that really run your staff. Not paychecks or shiny incentives. As I mentioned earlier, although money is great and certainly important, it's not the real reason your staff work for you.

Thinking about my Bali friend's question now, back when I first started The Game Changers I did feel guilty if I wasn't the hardest worker in the team.

Back then I actually had no choice to be the hardest worker anyway, because I hadn't systemised my business like you're learning to do in this book!

But even if my business didn't need me to work 60 hours a week, I would have.

Because the self-worth and self-image I had for myself, deep down, was driving my behaviour.

I saw myself from an employee mindset. 'More work equals more reward.'

Just like Pete, I was thinking at an $100 per hour level.

In an entrepreneur's mindset, less work and more thinking equals more reward. The more time I spend thinking, and feeling, and creating, the better my business performs.

That's $10,000 an hour thinking.

The more you can create $10,000 an hour ideas, the more you can reinvest in things that make their jobs easier, more enjoyable, and more valuable, so they don't want to leave.

Also, the more time you spend on creative problem solving, intuitive thinking, and implementing high-level improvements, the faster your business will evolve.

Earlier in my business, every time I'd step out, the business would turn into a poorly functioning circus. It would be absolutely chaotic.

And so, every time I left, I was abdicating responsibility to my team. Which put more pressure on them, and made their jobs a lot harder.

Whereas now I have the systems and processes, the business runs as easily and as smoothly if I was there or not. In many ways, it often runs smoother when I'm not there.

When I get back involved with the detail these days, I tend to create too many problems because I mess with the mix that's already happening.

I'm not on top of the finer details of the team, their capacity, their responsibilities, and where they're at.

That's what my Integrator is for.

And she's so ingrained with where the team's at, their capacity and how resourced they are, she decides what goes on when, and to who.

She loves the job, she loves working the hours that she works, she loves being involved in the team and having all that stuff going on. That's where she's at, that's her skillset.

As I talked about in chapter 6, you've got to have the right people in the right seats. Everybody needs to operate in their own wheelhouse.

We've covered a lot in this chapter. We've traveled through the last decades of business, learned that your staff have core needs (who would've thought?), outlined a better way to run weekly meetings, and discussed how to deal with resistance and guilt.

Here's what I want you to do next.

Organize to have your team's DISC profiles done.

Download our 'Needs Workbook' and brainstorm ways you can meet your team's 6 core needs.

Download our 'Winning the Week' meetings template, and start running your meetings in accordance with the rhythm set out.

You can do all three things at www.pathtofreedom.com.au/resources.

YOUR MINDSET

YOUR MINDSET

"Your business cannot outgrow you. The belief system you currently have is what's giving you your current results. To get different results… things have to change. YOU have to change."

Barry Magliarditi

The Game Changers' vision is to help people achieve the life of their dreams.

Sure, business is a major contributor to that outcome. But anyone can make a million bucks a year and still feel like rubbish every day because their health is terrible, their relationships are failing, and work is the only thing that gives them meaning in life.

As I said at the beginning of this book, your business is a vehicle for helping you achieve the lifestyle you want. Ideally, that's a lifestyle where all your needs are met - physical, mental, and spiritual.

To illustrate this, coaches use a tool called 'the Wheel of Life'. It's basically a pie chart with each section representing a part of a balanced life. Pieces include health, fun, love, work, growth, connection, and so on.

If your pie chart is out of balance, for example, your 'work' slice takes up 80% of the pie and the other 20% is for everything else…you're not living a balanced life, and total fulfillment will elude you. My wish for you is to

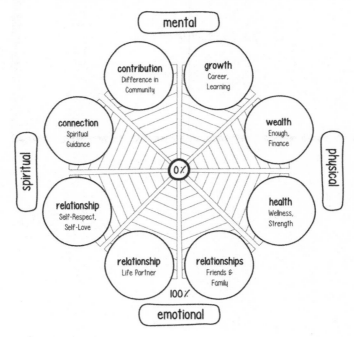

have a holistically balanced life. To have equal-sized slices of your pie. To have plentiful resources for all of the things that are important for your physical, mental, and spiritual health.

As we draw nearer to the end of this book, that's what I want you to start thinking about. When you've got all the pieces of your business working autonomously, and you're heading towards your ultimate vision... what else needs to happen to balance your life? So you can truly live the life of your dreams?

You might be wondering what all this has to do with mindset.

The answer? <u>Everything</u>.

In this chapter, instead of rolling out the same mindset pep talk you can find anywhere on Google, I want to dive deeper into what fuels the mindset you'll need to achieve the life of your dreams.

We're going to take a look behind the curtain, so to speak, and discover what's really pulling our strings.

But first, a quick primer...

Why is mindset so important?

As I've just mentioned, a successful life is about much more than money. But I'm going to use money as a yardstick to illustrate my first point.

Do you remember when you had your first $5k month? If you're like me, you were filled with excitement and energy. Five grand felt like an incredible achievement, especially because I had created it using my own smarts and hard work.

If you'd asked me then to consider what it would take to hit $50k a month - I would've quietly freaked out.

How much more pressure will I be under?
Can I handle the pace?
Can I handle the responsibility?

Can I handle the risk?

Obviously I had some very big goals. But I had little concept of how I would actually get there. I was a $5k month guy. Then as I continued to learn and grow, I became a $10k month guy. And so on…

Every 'level' you hit in business requires you to evolve into a person that can solve a different set of problems.

The mindset of a $10k a month person cannot handle what it takes to earn $100k a month. It's a whole new level of challenge and risk. You cannot expect a 10-year-old to beat Carl Lewis in the 100-meter sprint. Athletes like Carl Lewis train for years to be able to win gold in that race.

In your business, you need to train too. Not just your level of skill at running the business itself… but your mindset too.

Because even with the systems in place to create a business that works without you… eventually you WILL plateau if you're not consistently elevating your attitudes and beliefs.

Your business cannot outgrow you. The belief system you currently have is what's giving you your current results. To get different results… things have to change.

The kicker is… you don't know what's out there. If you're making $10k a month, you have no idea what it's like to make $100k a month.

To your subconscious mind, the unknown is pretty scary. It's 'unsafe'. But you cannot stay in your safe zone. Because you're not completely fulfilled there. The things you *really* want are sitting somewhere out there, in the unknown zone.

If you were completely satisfied with where you are right now in life, you wouldn't have picked up this book. I know you want more than you have now. More money, more love, more accomplishment… or all of the above.

To get more, you need to keep stretching beyond your comfort zone into the unknown zone.

That means being OK with risk. With failure. With adopting new ideas.

Now, I'm not going to continue this chapter by rehashing other stuff you've probably read ten times before.

Have a growth mindset.

Value progress over perfection.

Embrace failure.

And so on...

Don't get me wrong - that is all crucial. But you can easily find plenty of information about these concepts online. And I'm betting you've heard it all before anyway.

So let's look deeper.

Knowing you need to work on your mindset is one thing. But how do you actually *do* that? One just doesn't wake up one day and decide they're going to adopt a different set of beliefs and attitudes. If it were that easy, everyone would be walking around as their most evolved selves.

The issue is, the forces that drive our thoughts and actions are far more powerful - and hidden - than most people realize. Which is why we often get stuck in patterns that aren't giving us the results we want... yet we can't seem to break free of them.

Living our fullest potential in life begins with our mindset. Mindset creates behavior. Behavior creates results.

But what creates our mindset? Where does *that* come from?

Simply put: your mindset is an integration of the three drivers behind everything you do - mind, body, and spirit.

I'm about to peel back the layers and shine a light on what really drives the way we think, feel, and act.

Once you understand these drivers, you can begin your journey to achieving your full potential and living the life of your dreams.

And that's what this game called life is all about, isn't it?

Where do beliefs come from?

As human beings, we take on board what's typically known in the coaching space as belief-based patterning. Many coaches believe this begins when we're born. But I believe our belief systems start forming even earlier than that.

In my own experience working with hundreds of people in this space, I've witnessed people remember things from their first trimester of life. This may seem pretty out there, but science has actually uncovered many people who have prenatal memories. Famous sci-fi author Ray Bradbury claimed he could remember every detail of being born, from his head being crushed to suddenly being surrounded by bright lights.

In any case, a baby's brain forms 700 new neural connections every second. So it's crazy to think there's not a lot of very early programming going on from its experiences in the womb. Whether we remember it or not.

Given a baby's vulnerability and newness to life, it's no surprise that early belief-based patterning is about safety.

When we are young, we're trying to work out the world at a really fast pace.

What's OK? What's not OK? If I do this, what happens?

To survive, we have to make quick judgments based on the consequences of our experiences.

Sticking my hand on the hot kettle hurts, don't do that again. That's a 'bad' experience.

Sharing my toys gets me praise from my parent. Do that again. That's a good experience.

Poking the dog makes it growl which is scary. Don't do that again. That's a bad experience.

It seems simple enough, but when you dip beneath the surface of conscious thought, there are many decisions being made and beliefs being formed that we're not even aware of.

The negative impact of experiences like poking a growling dog can cause us to form a belief that isn't helpful. 'That experience was bad. Therefore, dogs are bad. I should be afraid of all dogs.'

Or, 'Sharing my toys was a good experience. People like it when I give everything away. So therefore I should always be overly generous and never want anything for myself.'

A common example is from back when many of us were toddlers, and we asked for something from our parents... and they yelled at us.

Back then we didn't have the capacity to understand why that was happening. We didn't know that our parents were just having a bad day, or whatever else was really going on with them. But we had to make a quick decision about whether asking for something had good or bad consequences.

Given we just had a bad experience after asking for something, we decided that we couldn't ask for what we wanted. And then we developed a belief around that, to keep us 'safe'.

As adults, this belief plays out as being unable to ask for what we really want. In relationships, at work, and even from ourselves.

Pretty much all of our earlier beliefs are created this way.

Stimulus + response = interpretation of what that means.

Growing into adulthood, many of these childhood beliefs don't serve us anymore. Crying to get what we want doesn't look good at the supermarket checkout. Withdrawing from affection to reassert control in a relationship doesn't make a happy home either.

Every response we give as adults, every belief we have, was built through 1000s of repetitions from childhood, into adolescence, and into adulthood.

That's why our results always align with our deepest beliefs.

If we believe we don't deserve to be financially wealthy – we'll hit a revenue plateau. If we don't believe we are deserving of love – we attract relationships that don't match our needs.

If we believe 'business is hard' – we create work (busyness) for ourselves that makes us work 80 hours a week on 'stuff'. If we believe we can't find good staff, we'll attract people who prove that bias right.

A lot of the time, we don't even realize we have these deep beliefs that are holding us back. How many times have you shook your head and said to yourself, 'Now *why* did I do that?'

Why do you keep doing the things you do?
Why do you keep having the experiences you have?

You still do it because it's your subconscious patterning playing out. It's your subconscious mind reacting to stimuli in alignment with the beliefs and patterns you established long ago.

Your subconscious mind will keep recreating these situations until you resolve them.

This is why I absolutely believe that you can put all the other steps in place to create a business that can run without you. You can hire mentors, you can create systems, you can build a good team.

But unless you address *you* as the founder of the business, *you* as the energetic being that birthed this thing... the business will never outgrow you.

We never have business problems, we have personal problems reflected in our business.

I wholeheartedly believe this. And I've seen evidence of this belief hundreds of times throughout my coaching career.

Remember Justin from chapter 11? How he couldn't find a good hire... partly because his job ad wasn't written to attract the right person? Remember that the second thing holding him back was his unconscious belief that he couldn't find anyone as good as him?

We had a coaching session to change his mindset. I helped him to step into a version of him that was open to hiring new team members, and voila, within a few weeks he hired a great employee.

Another client once came to me and said, "Barry we've been growing steadily financially, but this month we're at $50k. We're well below where we should be at $80k for the month. What can I do?"

So we ran a session, and uncovered some beliefs and some blockages that related back to the financial situation of his family as he was growing up. He was subconsciously holding back because of familial guilt about making a lot of money.

We broke through those beliefs, and within 24 hours he'd closed $252,000 worth of business. Which was more business than he'd ever closed in a month at that point.

I've seen it time and time again.

We get what we ask for. But most of the time, people aren't fully aware of what they're really asking.

How to resolve limiting beliefs

This takes some work most people would call 'soul searching'. But it's got nothing to do with sitting on a mountain and singing kumbaya. It's work best done in meditation, in quiet reflection, or with the guidance of an NLP-certified coach.

First, you need to identify the belief you want to address. For many, this is the hardest part. After all, beliefs become so well-ingrained that we don't even notice they are there. They're blind spots.

While a coaching session with an NLP-certified coach is probably the fastest and easiest way to do this, it is possible to identify your blind spots on your own.

First, think of a problem you're having.

Then try to peel back the layers and find the core belief that is stopping you from resolving that problem. Keep drilling down into your heart of hearts until you have your *aha* moment.

When you have identified the belief that is blocking you, it's time to go back through your memories to pinpoint the experience (or series of experiences) that caused you to form that belief in the first place.

When you revisit these experiences and analyze them from an adult perspective, you gain an understanding of how to break the pattern. Shadows cannot exist in the light.

Breaking the pattern is simply a matter of giving your younger self the experience you wanted, instead of the experience that birthed your unhelpful belief.

This can look like giving your 5-year-old self the love it didn't get from its parents.

Or like giving your 16-year-old self the forgiveness it needed from a friend.

Maybe you need to give your 8-year-old self permission to break free of family patternings.

When we give our old self the experience it needed, it grows up. The pattern gets resolved. The binding belief carries no emotion. We can put it aside and move on as the adult we want to be.

Most importantly, we start to create a new path in our neurology and literally change our thinking.

This coaching work is a bigger subject for my next book. But just know that beliefs can be changed, if you're willing to look at them, unpack them, and resolve them with the former version of you that created it.

Understanding self-sabotage

At the beginning of 2020, I was living in Bali. One of my goals while living there was to learn to surf. I practiced every day.

About a week before I left to come home to Australia to spend school holidays with my two sons, my surfboard rubbed the skin off the big toe on my right foot. I put some disinfectant on it, and within the week it was healed.

The day before my flight home, I stubbed the big toe on my *left* foot. Once again, the skin came off. Having just successfully resolved my last toe injury with some disinfectant, I hardly thought twice about the issue. I dabbed some disinfectant on my toe, and didn't think about it much thereafter.

After I came back to Australia… that damn toe just wouldn't heal.

I was still treating it with disinfectant. I didn't go to the doctor because I was in quarantine due to Coronavirus restrictions. I just thought, *'this thing will heal, it will be okay'*.

So I kept repeating the pattern of behavior I had used before to heal my other toe.

But I wasn't getting the results I wanted. Every day, the toe would seem to get better. And then the next morning I would wake up to find it red, sore, and full of yellow pus.

Still I didn't change my pattern of belief and behavior. I just soaked it in salt water, and put disinfectant on it, and cleaned out the gunk. "It'll be okay tomorrow."

Until eventually one morning I woke up in severe pain. I also had a lump in my groin.

Finally, I accepted that I had to change something. The pattern of my previous toe injury experience was not repeating here. So I went to see a doctor. Not surprisingly, he told me I had a severe infection.

The doctor spent some time cleaning up the wound on the *outside*. Then he gave me some antibiotics for the infection on the *inside*.

Sure enough, within 24 hours, the infection and swelling had gone down. And within two days the enlarged gland in my groin had resolved. Within a week the thing healed up and the issue was over.

Why am I telling you this stomach-churning story?

To illustrate that we are so shaped by previous experiences, we can easily ignore what new data is telling us.

Mindset is such a strong controlling force, most people will walk off a cliff rather than change their beliefs and behaviors.

So what's really at play here? Why do we keep holding onto beliefs that aren't helping us get the outcomes we want? Why do we self-sabotage?

Reptilian brain neurology

If we look back through our evolution, earlier humans didn't have the same brain structure that we do now. We were operating out of different neurology.

We still have an archaic part of our brain that is 100% focused on survival. I introduced our 'critter brain' at the beginning of this book. It's technically called our reptilian brain. Our reptilian brain is involved with primitive drives such as hunger, thirst, and reproduction. Thinking back to Maslow's Hierarchy of Needs, the reptilian brain is responsible for the bottom level - survival.

Although these days we live in houses with lockable windows and doors and roofs, and there are no saber-toothed tigers hanging around, to our reptilian brain, modern-day threats are just as scary as being eaten.

Threats like failure. Embarrassment. Shame. Our reptilian brain does everything it can to make us avoid these thoroughly unpleasant situations. Even though doing so hinders our growth - failure is an essential part of being an entrepreneur.

In fact, the more you're willing to fail, the more you're likely to succeed.

The problem is, to our reptilian brain, the experiences that we learn to survive growing up become the experiences that it believes our continued survival depends upon.

So if we have survived experiences of poverty, of poor health, or toxic relationships... they've all been pre-programmed as *survivable*. We unconsciously seek out and repeat these experiences. Because our reptilian brain has marked them as 'safe'.

This becomes a problem if we haven't had the experience of being wealthy. Our reptilian brain says, 'Woah there, hang on. This is uncharted territory. It could be dangerous. You don't know if you can survive this experience. Better not go there!'

So we self-sabotage.

The same goes for relationships. Or weight-loss regimes. Or a hundred other things we get stuck on. We repeat the patterns of our parents. Or our grandparents.

I actually believe our behavior and information is passed to us from earlier generations through our DNA. This may be how we inherit generational emotional baggage.

Have you ever caught yourself doing something in a relationship and thought, 'Oh my god. I sound just like my dad!'?

That's because you're learned his behavioral patterns. And you haven't questioned them. You haven't done the mindset work needed to unpack your belief system, backtrack to where your beliefs were formed, and consciously decide which beliefs are helping you achieve what you want in life, and which are not.

It's not always easy - when dealing with the reptilian brain, you're going against around 10 million years of evolution. But there are some really effective ways to reprogram your belief system using neuro-linguistic programming (NLP) and other psychology-based modalities.

I won't get into them here, because that's a topic for another book. Maybe my next one...

As with everything else in this book, if you would like to explore the topic further or experience this type of coaching for yourself, reach out to a Game Changers coach at www.pathtofreedom.com.au/go

Building your intuition

Spirituality has become a woo-woo term that many people like to scoff at these days.

But it's a core driver behind your mindset and emotional state. Spirituality forms a big part of the inner guidance, the instinct, the *intuition* that drives our beliefs and behaviors. Call it God, Allah, Gaia, nature, spirit, or just the energy from the Universe, I believe there is a source that we are all tapped into. And we access it through connection with our heart.

We all have that feeling or voice we can't put our finger on that guides us through life. An inner guidance that seemingly comes from nowhere. But in fast-paced, unforgiving modern life, most people don't listen to theirs... at least, not as much as they should.

This intuition grows stronger, and more reliable, the more you connect with it. The more you align your heart and mind to cultivate a higher level of intuitive living.

When we're born, we haven't yet developed our brain, or our logic, or our understanding of life. Yet babies have an intuition, a knowing. It goes beyond instinct and into something deeper.

Mothers have their own intuition too. Soon after their baby is born, new mums intuitively know how to care for their baby, even though it might be their first child.

Kids also have this uncanny ability to know the difference between right and wrong. Sure, they push the boundaries... but they innately know where those boundaries are.

Sure, you can say, 'well, the baby is operating through instinct.' Or, 'kids pick up on cues we don't even see'. While that's certainly true, it explains what's going on in the *brain*. Intuition is about the *heart*.

After all, following our brain doesn't always work out...

Perhaps you've had experiences in life where you've had big decisions to make, and you've felt the right decision in your heart, yet logically it never stacked up. So you chose to follow your brain. And things went bad.

Or vice versa - maybe you followed your intuition once, even when your brain was telling you it was the wrong choice... but things actually worked out better than you could have expected.

Intuition is our connection to a source, into a deeper knowing, and a deeper alignment to the journey that we're here to embark upon in life.

A mentor once told me that significant issues happen to us when we're not listening to our inner guidance. I've certainly found this to be true in my life.

Back when I went bankrupt in my earlier business, although part of me wanted to blame something other than myself... I knew that experience was a lesson for me.

And even though it was a terribly traumatic experience, I know now that there was a purpose behind it. Because that experience was the doorway to me starting to understand psychology, NLP, looking into quantum physics, and discovering the mind.

So this is why when I look at my own journey, I see the journey as looking *inwards* as opposed to looking outwards.

All the answers lie within us. Answers to our questions, to our problems... it's all within our heart. Our mind, when it's repeating old unhelpful patterns, just confuses and distorts the message.

Thinking back to my pus-filled toe...

My toe was trying to get rid of something that was inside it causing infection. It was giving me signs that something wasn't right.

Yet I didn't listen. I bandaged the outside, but I didn't address what was happening on the inside until it got really bad.

This is what happens with most people.

They don't address their relationship issues until their third divorce. Or they don't do something about their health until they are diagnosed with type 2 type diabetes. They won't explore their self-worth and identity issues until a mid-life crisis brings their world crashing down.

Experiences keep repeating until we resolve them. The more you connect to your heart, and develop your intuition for your path forward, the easier - and more fulfilling - your journey will be.

Changing your mindset

From early childhood, we each build our self-identity in order to operate within our familial and social circles. We do this both consciously and unconsciously.

I am honest. I am clever. I am funny.

I am a wife. I am a brother. I am a coach.

I am a runner. I am a cat lover. I am an artist.

Our self-identity is probably the biggest influencer of our mindset. But here's where that can get tricky...

Our subconscious mind always wants to be congruent with our thoughts and beliefs. So it will keep creating experiences that prove us right.

If at our core we believe that we're unworthy, we're going to consciously and unconsciously attract experiences that validate that belief.

If at our core we believe we're not deserving of love, we're going to choose partners that don't meet our emotional needs.

If at our core we believe we're 'dumb' because we didn't finish school or go to uni, we're going to sabotage our business when things get bigger than we think we can handle.

And so on.

Changing your mindset is not a matter of saying mantras 100 times a day.

If you have an experience, a belief, an unconscious family loyalty, or something sitting deep inside of you that's unresolved... no mantra is going to stick.

Sure, you might start to experience some aspect of moving towards your new belief if you're pounding it into your head 100 times a day. But it's not sustainable. It won't last. You cannot create change by sheer force of will - just think of every failed diet you've ever tried!

Changing your mindset involves addressing your self-identity.

Who do you really believe you are? And how is that self-image influencing your behavior and results in life?

Do you do everything yourself because you inherently don't trust others?

Do you sabotage your earnings because you don't believe you are worthy of wealth?

Do you resist change because you secretly like being the hardest working underdog?

Food for thought...

Most people don't spend the time to question themselves. They're so busy trying to do things on the outside. Make money, hire the right staff, be a strong leader, attract good leads... all that stuff is what I call the 'outer game'.

But the real transformative work is done on the inside, on your 'inner game'.

With that said, it's time to identify the core beliefs about *your* self-identity that are holding you back from activating your true potential and living the life of your dreams.

And it's time to step into a new version of yourself.

As this chapter's 'homework', I want you to journal on these three questions:

> Who do you believe you are, deep down inside?

> Who are you pretending to be to the outside world?

> What's the self-created story you keep playing out?

Get out a pen, or open up your laptop, and just start writing from the heart.

Journal every day if you can. It takes discipline to get started, especially if you're the kind of person who doesn't practice self-reflection often (or at all).

But the deep beliefs you have about yourself are shaping your life right now.

They'll shape your future, too.

The more you journal, and the more honest you are, the more you will get out of the exercise. It's only *after* you identify unhelpful beliefs and patterns that you can start charting a more fulfilling path forward. It doesn't work the other way around.

I get that this probably isn't what you expected from this chapter.

I'm sure you didn't expect to be told to journal on your identity to help uncover the subconscious beliefs that drive your behavior and results.

When you picked up this book, you probably just wanted the steps. You wanted to do, do, do.

"Just give me the strategies Barry!"

The strategies you've learned in this book WILL change your business.

But this chapter will change your life.

THE PATH TO FREEDOM

ENTREPRENEUR

ENTREPRENEUR

"Being an entrepreneur is an expression. It's almost like art. Its creating something out of nothing. It's a journey of transformation within yourself. It brings up your shit and challenges your passion and drive. Every new level has a new level of challenge built-in - you cannot progress unless you grow with it."

Clint X Morgan

"I think I'm on this planet to do something really huge."

I was at the gym, and on the phone with my friend Clint.

"What are you thinking, mate?" I asked him.

"I might start an online group teaching people how to make a living online."

Clint always had an entrepreneurial spirit. But for a long time, his ability to create the freedom he dreamt of was blocked by a really bad relationship with money.

He had worked a 9-5 life and had some success. He'd become a personal trainer and realized how much he enjoyed helping people. He'd tried a few money-making ventures online. But still, nothing quite fit.

Back when I first met Clint, he was perpetually broke and lacking direction. But he was hungry for something more, and was searching for that special spark. Searching for his life's purpose, perhaps.

During that conversation in the gym, I sensed he was on the cusp of something important. "Do it mate," I urged him. "See what happens."

So he did.

Clint invested heavily in his personal development, surrounded himself with mentors, and went 'all-in' with his business. His first workshop had about 30 people. 18 months later, he was presenting to a group of 900 raving fans.

Fast forward to now, Clint is the perfect example of entrepreneurial success. He's running multiple successful companies and has created a mass movement behind his mission.

Locationally and financially independent, Clint and his wife and child travel the world, running the business from their laptop wherever they happen to be.

Like all worthwhile things in life, it wasn't easy.

"Before I started my journey in business, I was really timid," he told me when we caught up recently to record an interview for my podcast, The Comeback Game.

"I'd shrink myself down to fit in. I was afraid to talk to people and speak my truth. I couldn't talk to a woman I liked to save myself. And if you had asked me to get on stage and speak to 1,000 people, I would have had a panic attack."

"I cannot imagine you like that," I laughed. "What changed things for you?"

"After I started reading business books like 'Think and Grow Rich', 'The Magic of Thinking Big', 'How to Win Friends and Influence People', and so on, I noticed something that changed everything for me."

I leaned in, eager to hear Clint's realization.

"I found that while those books helped me learn about business, the personal development lessons within them had a much more profound effect on how I felt and presented to the world.

"I realized that I could become anyone if I just learned the process behind it," Clint continued. "I could become confident speaking to hundreds of people. I could become a more secure and strong partner. I could literally change myself. I'd never imagined that before - I just thought that the way you were, was the way you would always be."

"That's incredible," I smiled. "So the skills you were picking up as an entrepreneur were transferable to your life."

"Yeah. And the better entrepreneur I became, the better person I became too."

What does it mean to be an entrepreneur?

According to the dictionary, an entrepreneur is 'a person who sets up a business or businesses, taking on financial risks in the hope of profit'.

What a dreary summary. And not very exciting either. 'In the *hope* of profit'? How depressing.

Having lived an entrepreneur's life for the past 18 years, I can tell you that being an entrepreneur is much more than that.

Reading this book as an entrepreneur yourself (or wanting to be one), you probably have a different experience of what it means too.

Maybe your experience of entrepreneurship is working 80+ hours a week and going 'all in' to build your dream. Or maybe it's taking baby steps as you try to get your fledgling business off the ground.

You might be already successful, but want to run things more efficiently while reducing your work hours. Perhaps you've hit entrepreneur paydirt - you've sold your business, and are looking for your next challenge.

Wherever you are in your journey, I'm sure you can attest that being an entrepreneur is not so much something you *do*... but something that you *are*.

We are mavericks that buck society's status quo.

We are obsessed with building our dreams.

We are resilient and courageous.
And we will never stop.

Whether your vision is a simple dream of providing for your family or a large-scale world-changer, as an entrepreneur **you're one of the most important people on the planet.**

We make new things happen.

We ask 'what else is possible?'

We contribute to a better world.

The beauty of being an entrepreneur is that you get to make your own rules. You get to shape your life how you want.

The limits that society puts on 'normal' people's lives… they don't exist for you. There's no 'ceiling' on what you can achieve.

Make what you want. Do what you want. Live how you want.

The journey isn't always easy. But when you master the basics, it's a whole lot of fun.

This is our last chapter together (for this book at least…)

So let's use our remaining time to take a deeper look at what being an entrepreneur really means, and how to be a successful one.

Developing your personal power

In February 2020, I was living in Bali at the beginning of what was to be a year of growth, reflection, and discovery. That is, until Coronavirus hit… but that's another story for another time.

I remember sitting one day at a table in one of my favorite cafes in Canggu. I had just signed off on a Zoom meeting with my team and was hit with a really powerful realization.

I was kind of obsolete.

My team was running my business for me. And doing a damn good job of it.

It was a moment of true pride and a feeling of, 'Wow, I'm living what I teach. I can step in and out of my business as I choose.'

In that moment, I reflected on my leadership ability. How had I been able to influence this group of people to run my business for me at such a high standard?

Twelve months prior, I really felt I was a terrible leader. Because although my business was profitable and growing, everything to do with staff felt like a struggle.

I knew that as a leader, the performance of my team (or lack thereof) was on me. Our business is a reflection of ourselves. I knew I was both the problem and the solution.

So I spent 2019 working on my leadership ability. I wanted to become a better leader for my team. Not just because that makes my business better, but because The Game Changers' vision applies to my team just like everybody else - I want *them* to activate their truest potential and live the life of their dreams too.

Sitting back in that café in Bali, reflecting on my A-team, I realized something important. I had previously assumed this thing called leadership was something that focused *outwards*. It was about conversations. Meetings. And so on.

But my leadership had improved not because I'd learned how to have different conversations with my staff. It improved because I'd learned to have different conversations with *myself*.

As I often say, I don't believe people have business problems. They have personal problems that are expressed through their business.

Similarly to how Clint's unhealthy relationship with money crippled his earlier business building efforts, some of my old mindset patterns used to play out in my business too.

I used to get so heavily triggered by problems that it prevented me from leading my team in a resourceful way. I let the things that were happening around me dictate my reactions… which in turn affected the people I was trying to influence.

How can we grow our business to its fullest potential if we are not also growing to our fullest potential as people?

How can we develop others, if we're constantly giving your own power away by reacting to the world, instead of controlling our responses to it?

The success of your efforts as an entrepreneur largely relates to your ability to influence others. The more your business grows, the more people you'll need to run it for you.

And you cannot lead your team resourcefully if problems, situations, or comments set you off into a spiral of doubt, frustration, fear, anger, or hopelessness.

That's where your level of personal power comes in.

According to Robert Firestone, PhD in his book The Ethics of Interpersonal Relationships, there are two forms of power, negative and positive. This is how he describes it -

Personal power is based on strength, confidence, and competence that individuals gradually acquire in the course of their development. It is self-assertion, and a natural, healthy striving for love, satisfaction and meaning in one's interpersonal world.

This type of power represents a movement toward self-realization and transcendent goals in life; its primary aim is mastery of self, not others.

Personal power is more an attitude or state of mind than an attempt to maneuver or control others. It is based on competence, vision, positive personal qualities, and service. When externalized it is likely to be more generous, creative, and humane than other forms of power.

I believe that as entrepreneurs - and as human beings - we all need to develop our level of personal power. It starts with personal responsibility - accepting that we are absolutely 100% accountable for the way that we respond to any given situation.

We give our personal power away in many subtle ways. As an entrepreneur, that sucks away your ability to create the results you crave.

Do you feel a sense of being stuck?

Do you feel tired, resentful, frustrated, or angry?
Do you feel that things are out of your control?

It's your responsibility to clean that stuff up. To work on your *inner game* and develop your internal locus of control. Because any time that you react negatively or get triggered, you're giving away your power to someone else, or to the situation itself.

This leaves you feeling weak and vulnerable… which is pretty much the opposite of the emotional and mental state you need when trying to change the world!

On the flip side, stepping into your own personal power involves accepting personal responsibility for your actions and your results. Of practicing forgiveness. Approaching situations with openness and curiosity. Knowing your values and establishing healthy boundaries.

People who embrace their own personal power have a heightened ability to influence people. Think Barack Obama. Oprah Winfrey. Tony Robbins.

Without developing your own personal power, you're in for a rough time as an entrepreneur. Because a big part of your job is influencing people. You need to build other leaders to do the things you don't have the skill or resources to do.

Will you give your power to everything that happens outside yourself? Or will you be the only one who determines your thoughts, feelings, actions, and results?

Business is never a smooth ride. There are going to be challenges. Problems. Stuff-ups. Disappointments. You cannot control that. The only thing you can do is control how you react to them.

So take control. If you're not sure how to start, a Game Changers coach may be able to help. Reach out at www.pathtofreedom.com.au/go

Your responsibility as an entrepreneur

I believe as entrepreneurs, we have the ability to change the world. Much more so than the politicians and leaders of the country. We have the ability to impact, influence, and change the world through the products and services we bring to life.

Think of artists and creators who have changed life as we know it.

J.K. Rowling, Estee Lauder, Walt Disney.

Thomas Edison, Steve Jobs, Henry Ford.

These people that pushed the limitations of what the world said they could do. They chose not to say 'no'.

Think of how different the world would be if the Wright brothers accepted that people could not fly.

If Magellan accepted that the world was flat.

If Thomas Edison accepted that harnessing light was impossible.

If Charles Babbage - the inventor of the first mechanical computer - accepted that machines could not 'think'.

I'm not saying that your dreams need to be this big and world-changing. Maybe they are, I don't know. But right now you're doing something that an earlier version of you thought was not possible. Every single day, you're inventing something new for yourself. You're inventing a new way of thinking, working, and living.

It's because people have chosen not to settle for the status quo that we live in the world we live in today. It's because people have chosen not to take on board the beliefs of society and the old ways of doing things, that we are where we are.

It's thanks to entrepreneurs who chose to tap into their intuition. They chose to create a new path instead of following the same one others were walking.

The car wasn't created because Henry Ford simply thought of it as a good idea. Henry had an intuition, a belief of what was possible. And he persisted with his vision, even when everyone said it would never work.

As an entrepreneur, you are also breaking through the impossible. Whether on a small scale or a large one, it doesn't matter. You are paving the path to a new future, every day.

To me, that's pretty exciting.

But to many others, it's terrifying. Maybe it's terrifying to you too sometimes.

Which brings me to my point.

As entrepreneurs, we have to be okay with being all of who we are.

I'm not even talking about the concept of business right now. I'm talking about you owning your God-given right to be who you are on this planet. Different. A round peg in a square hole.

Being an entrepreneur is about you being fully self-expressed.

It's about speaking and living your truth.

It's about saying, 'Okay, what I'm doing might trigger some people. Other people might not support me or believe in me. But it won't deter me from reaching my goals.'

Some people might leave you. Some friends or family won't get what you're doing. Or they subconsciously won't want you to grow and change, because that threatens to disrupt how they like things to be.

But if you're clear on who you are, and people choose to leave you, they were never supporters of who you really are in the first place. They were supporters of who you were pretending to be.

And that's energy that you don't want or need around you. Because believe me, it will hold you back. Even if you don't realize it at the time.

In my own circle, I've got people that love me, and support me, and back me, no matter what. And I've also got people that challenge the hell out of me, but would still pick me up if I fell over.

There's a difference between those people and others who cut you down. Who don't accept and love you for who you are - even if they don't agree with everything you do.

Know which is which.

Stepping up and leaning in

This book was written during a pandemic. Heavy COVID-19 restrictions have put millions of people out of work worldwide.

The world was already seeing a rise in entrepreneurship before Coronavirus hit. But now in 2020, entrepreneurship is hotter than ever. The search phrase 'how to start a business' gets 8,170,000,000 results in Google.

What people are really looking for is *freedom*.

They are looking for *liberation*.

They are trying to find a way to live without relying on someone else for their livelihood... because it can all get taken away so quickly.

And they're seeing entrepreneurship as a vehicle for that. After all, you can put up a website and start selling a product or service in just a day.

But entrepreneurship is so much more than just building a business.

As I said at the beginning of this chapter, being an entrepreneur is not a job or something you 'do'- it's a lifestyle. It's something you ARE.

It's about stepping into all of who you are, and realizing that if you were removed from the earth, there would be a tiny hole where you belong.

You have a right to be here. You have a right to make your time on this planet whatever you want it to be.

If you look at every single human being in all of existence lined up in a row, which one of those is not worthy of being themselves? Which one of those is not worthy of being all of who they're here to be?

The answer, of course, is none.

Every single person on this planet is worthy of being themselves. Of pursuing the goals and dreams that make them feel alive and give them purpose. No matter how outlandish or unachievable they might seem.

I believe that what stops us from being fully empowered to live the life that we want, is our inability to be all of who we are.

It's the continuance of living in false paradigms or belief systems that don't support who we really are, and what we're really here to do.

Have you ever felt that you needed to hold your true self back?

That if you said how you really feel, you'd be shunned?

That you don't have the right to pursue your dreams?

I want you to throw all that crap out of the window. Right now. Just get rid of it.

This is my permission slip for you, dear reader, to be *you*.

100% unashamedly, wholeheartedly, and authentically YOU.

All the bits. The crazy bits. The funny bits. The serious bits. The scary bits. They all make up who you are. And you deserve to wander through this world - and this life - living your truth.

Damn what society says.

To hell with friends or family who don't believe in you.
And screw all the naysayers who will try and stand in your way.

The world needs YOU.

Not some false version that you're pretending to be because it fits in with what your parents want from you, or what your friends want from you, or what that girlfriend wants from you…

If you're afraid of being criticized, or laughed at, or abandoned, to really step out and be you...

This is your permission to be all of who you're here to be.

To claim your power and share your true self with the world.

If you're waiting for a sign that you are supported and encouraged to be the highest version of yourself…

This is it.

Don't hold back. Don't dim your light. Don't be afraid of being all that you are, and all that you can be.

The world needs you.

Go get your dreams!

Where to from here?

I've had a great time writing this book. I hope you've had a great time reading it too.

Now it's up to you.

I have given you the steps for creating a business that runs without you.

I have shown you the path to freedom.

What you do with that information… is up to you.

Make the choice. Follow the steps. Do the work.

I've given you all the help I can along the way. You can access all the worksheets for each book chapter at this link: www.pathtofreedom.com.au/resources

If you're having difficulty doing it on your own, talk to a Game Changers coach. They will help you work out your Game Plan™ for rapid growth over the next 6-12 months and beyond.

Building a business that can run without you is easy when you follow the steps you've learned in this book. But it's also hard work.

At the beginning, you'll have to put in a lot of effort to get things up and running the way you want.

But if you keep consistently pushing forward, and implement the steps one by one, you WILL achieve the goal: A freedom business that fuels your dream lifestyle.

I've seen it happen time and again with our private coaching clients at The Game Changers. The members who embrace uncertainty, keep faith in the steps you've just learned, and don't give up always get incredible results.

They change their life. That's what I want for you too.

So make a start. Right now. Take action.

Knowledge is nothing unless you actually put it to work.

So take the first step - and start changing your Game.

About the Author

Barry Magliarditi is a business coach, entrepreneur, investor, author, speaker, and transformation specialist who has helped 1,000s of business owners earn more, work less, and create a life of fulfillment.

He is also the founder and director of The Game Changers, a company dedicated to helping people activate their truest potential and achieve personal freedom through business. The Game Changers helps entrepreneurs and business owners scale to 7 and 8-figures using battle-tested frameworks that unlock rapid growth and profit.

Barry started his first business, a kitchen and bathroom renovation company when he was 18 years old. The business scaled quickly and soon Barry was managing 15 staff and a multi-million dollar turnover.

But Barry's experience of success did not match his expectations. Instead of a life of financial and personal freedom, Barry found himself working 80+ hour weeks, feeling stressed and burned out, and watching his personal relationships disintegrate.

His business wasn't his vehicle for freedom - it was his prison.

After losing it all and hitting rock bottom, Barry knew in his heart that there had to be a way to create the business and lifestyle he dreamed of. He set about learning how to create a profitable and scalable business that provided sustainable growth and personal freedom.

Barry began his never-ending self-education journey through personal development, business, and spirituality. He learned quickly that the key to a holistically balanced and successful life is what's going on inside - our "inner game".

By working on his inner game, Barry was able to create tangible and sustainable results in his business. What's more, he was able to guide others to shift their *own* inner game and create remarkable positive change in their businesses and lives as well.

This was the catalyst that sparked the creation of The Game Changers.

Since 2012, Barry and The Game Changers team have helped business owners to create lifestyle businesses that give them the time, financial freedom, and personal fulfillment they dream of.

Barry has been recognized for his thought leadership by the 30 under 30 and the Telstra Business awards, and was chosen as Australian Coach of the Year in the 2016 Invia Innovation and Excellence in Business Coaching in Australia.

The Game Changers operate with the belief that professional success should not come at the cost of your family, your mental and physical health, or your personal life. Our definition of success is waking up every day feeling aligned with your purpose, doing what you love, and having the freedom to csnipphoose your path through life.

Barry Magliarditi and The Game Changers team are on a mission to help you unlock your truest potential.

If you're ready to take the next step towards tripling your profits, doubling your time off, and creating a life aligned with your wildest dreams, we'd love to hear from you.

Get in touch with a Game Changers coach at www.thepathtofreedom.com.au/go

Made in the USA
Las Vegas, NV
16 April 2022

47583071R00187